The Natural Presenter

Published in 2007 by
Institute of Chartered Accountants in Ireland
CA House, Pembroke Road
Ballsbridge, DUBLIN 4

Designed and typeset in Minion and Gill Sans by Marsha Swan
Printed by E-Print, Dublin
The paper used in the printing of this book was produced from managed, renewable, plantation forests.

ISBN 978 0 903854 28 3

The opinions expressed in this publication are those of the authors and do not necessarily represent the views of the ICAI. The text is designed to provide accurate and authoritative information in regard to the subject matter covered. It is sold on the understanding that the ICAI is not engaged in rendering professional services. If professional advice or other expert assistance is required, the services of a competent professional should be sought.

The Natural Presenter

Turning Conversations into Presentations

Barry Brophy

Institute of Chartered Accountants in Ireland
Dublin

For my parents.

CONTENTS

ACKNOWLEDGEMENTS

No book is even nearly the work of one person. I would like to thank the ICAI, and specifically Kieran Lyons, for investing his faith in this idea, and then seeing it through so swiftly and smoothly. I would also like to thank the people who did all of the things that I would never be able to do, so well, namely: Winifred Power, Marsha Swan, Niall McCormack, Agnieszka Pobedynska and Michael Brown. Working with them was, for me, the most interesting part of the whole project.

I would like to thank everyone who offered comment or advice, in particular my dad, who carried out a meticulous and extremely useful review at an important stage. I would especially like to thank Siobhán for encouraging the venture, unflappingly, from start to finish, and Seán McLoughney for suggesting that I stop considering writing and start writing.

Lastly, I would like to thank anyone who said anything encouraging. You would be surprised at how many of these comments are remembered, and how much energy they gave me.

INTRODUCTION: THE IMPORTANCE OF COMMUNICATION

The digital boom of the last twenty years has brought us into a business world that is increasingly specialised and a marketplace that is truly global. The need to communicate quickly and clearly has never been greater and a major part of this communication effort is concerned with speaking before groups of people. Acquiring the skills necessary to make presentations is an excellent way to lever real improvement in your place of work. It improves the transfer of information in-house, as well as making you a better representative for your company externally.

And yet, making presentations is, for many people, the most daunting and nerve-racking thing that they ever have to do. There is often a strong fear associated with speaking before a group but, by learning the basic principles of preparation and delivery, you can overcome these fears and present with confidence. When you do, it is tremendously rewarding.

You might be reading this and thinking that you would love to master these skills but you imagine that it involves a huge amount of work – it doesn't. You already have the skills necessary to present, all of them. They come from your palette of conversational skills and you have been practising these since you were very young, even before you could talk. These are the skills you will use, and the rest is just planning, preparation and a bit of imagination. You don't have to be a performer to make a presentation, you just have to know what you are talking about and then deliver this, in your own personal style, with conviction.

The main difference between this and other books is found in 'Part Four: Bridging the Gap'. There is always a gap between the knowledge of the presenter and that of the audience. It is this gap that necessitates the presentation in the first place. Techniques are introduced in this section for communicating to a range of different audiences. These are particularly useful for people who make technical presentations but are applicable to all. The psychological rationale behind the various points is also explored.

The book is divided into the following parts:

Part One: The Basics – This short section lists the top 12 problems facing a presenter, and then explains three important fundamentals that underpin everything else covered in the book.

Part Two: Preparation – This is concerned with all of the work you put in to prepare for the presentation and, in particular, with developing a logical structure. There is also a comprehensive chapter on visual aids.

Part Three: Delivery – How you deliver your material when you actually stand up to speak.

Part Four: Bridging the Gap – This part looks at how the expert presenter explains his or her ideas to the non-expert audience, a challenge that exists – to a greater or lesser extent – in all presentations.

Part Five: Bringing it All Together – This section looks at what you do before and after the presentation in order to maximise your success. Included is how to deal with questions, and a chapter devoted to lectures and wedding speeches.

Throughout the book there are exercises that you can use to put the various ideas into practice.

This book is for anyone who ever has to stand up and address a group. It will help you to think clearly about the challenges of making a presentation. Hopefully it will also show you that this task is not nearly as difficult as you might have thought. After that, it's over to you. With practise, anyone can master these skills and reap the personal and professional rewards to be gained from presenting well.

The Natural Presenter

PART ONE: THE BASICS

This section contains two short, but extremely important, chapters. The first summarises the main difficulties that presenters face: many of these will be obvious to the reader, but several will not be. It is important to realise that part of the problem is that presenters can be oblivious to many of their own faults. The second chapter sets down the most important guidelines for making any presentation, and these will be referred to throughout the book.

1. THE MAIN DIFFICULTIES

Listed below are the main problems that people encounter when making a presentation. Some of these, such as overcoming nerves, are all too apparent to the presenter. However, several will not be perceived as problems at all, and therein lies their significance. If you don't think that you have a problem, then you are unlikely to try to solve it.

1. Nerves – This is the most obvious difficulty. Everyone gets nervous about speaking in front of a group, many severely so. This topic is looked at in detail in Chapter 12. However, a large part of the solution is gained by not tackling the problem at all, but rather by preparing in a way that will eliminate most of the sources of the stress. This will be a recurring theme in 'Part Two: Preparation'.

2. Keeping the audience's attention – There is nothing more soul-crushing than watching an audience stretch, yawn, fidget and fall asleep in front of you. And these are only the obvious cases, as an audience will rarely be so bold as to tell you they are bored. Presenters wonder how they can make their material and their delivery more interesting, but to think this way is to miss an important point. Interesting delivery comes not from a bright style or positive body language, but rather a clear understanding of what the audience needs, and how you can meet this need. The way to keep attention is to have a clear aim (Chapter 2), to prepare in a sensible way (all of Part Two), and to use the engaging communication tools discussed in Part Four. 'Energy and Enthusiasm' (Chapter 10) will then be the icing on the cake for keeping your audience's attention.

3. Keeping it simple – It is a general truism that presenters usually fear being too simplistic, and audiences usually find them to be too complicated. What happens is that presenters forget what it was like not to know, and over-assume regarding what the audience can pick up from a briskly delivered oral presentation. This is discussed throughout the book, but particularly useful in addressing the problem are the use of analogies (Chapter 14) and examples (Chapter 15), as well as some of the insights discussed on mental bridging (Chapter 13).

4. Keeping it structured – All communications – films, television programmes, newspaper articles, instruction manuals, even phone calls –

require structure if a clear message is to be imparted. With this in mind, there is an in-depth look at structure in Chapter 5.

5. PowerPoint – The use of PowerPoint is a contentious issue. Like all digital tools, it brings potential benefits, but it is also open to abuse. On the one hand, the displaying of sophisticated graphics has never been more easy or less time-consuming; on the other, people have taken to putting everything they want to say onto their slides, which has become a distraction to the audience and, more dangerously, a distraction to the presenter, who often plays second fiddle to the slide-show. This issue will be dealt with in the chapter on visual aids (Chapter 7).

6. Graphs and diagrams – The issue of PowerPoint and what text you should put on to your slides is considered by most presenters but the graphs, diagrams and pictures they use rarely merit the same scrutiny. There is a reason for this: presenters can easily see what needs to be shown in a graphic. They automatically filter out the other details and the other possible interpretations of the slide, but the people in the audience may not be able to do this. Confusing or misleading graphics are one of the most common and damaging faults of all, particularly in technical presentations. There will be a detailed analysis of this, also in the chapter on visual aids (Chapter 7).

7. Adopting the right style – Unlike the issue of visual aids, to which too little thought is given, the issue of style is one where presenters try too hard to be many things that they aren't, and don't need to be. People turn themselves into newsreaders, politicians, even stand-up comedians, when their own natural style is by far the best to adopt. Why this is the case, and how you bring this style – in all its colour – to the podium will be explored in the chapter on conversing with the audience (Chapter 9).

8. Getting off to a good start – How many times have you heard presenters say that they felt very nervous until they got going, but then they were fine? The start is not only a big obstacle for the presenter but also for the audience. You want them to get interested in what you're saying as soon as possible. The difficult business of getting off to a good start is looked at in the section on introductions in Chapter 5, and some of the tools mentioned here are then explored in greater detail in 'Part Four: Bridging the Gap'.

9. Not losing your way – Everyone worries about the room going out of focus and their mind going blank. The way to avoid this, or recover from it if it happens, is to have a good set of guide notes to work from (Chapter 6) and also to have a sensible structure, which is not a long set of facts, propositions and bullet-points, but rather a short set of easily explained and easily remembered chunks (such as examples and stories). This will also be dealt with in Part Four of the book.

10. Making the delivery crisp – Many presentations are dull and monotonic, while others may be hectic and rushed. You must strike a balance between keeping your delivery fresh and varied, and yet well controlled and easy on the ear. These two aspects – fresh delivery, and controlled delivery – will be looked at in chapters 9 and 10.

11. Body language – Like the problem of adopting the right style, this is a problem only because people perceive it to be a problem, and then make misguided attempts to address it. Simply put: body language is the biggest red herring of presenting, as most of the time it takes care of itself, and to focus your attention on it directly only distracts you. Ironically, it is such a big non-issue that it merits a chapter of its own (Chapter 11) to set the record straight.

12. Making it memorable – This is another of the faults that the majority of presenters are completely ignorant of. Most people have a very poor understanding of what the audience will remember from a presentation. The simple answer is: very little. However, if you have some insight into what *is* memorable, it will help you to design the presentation so that the key points remain in the minds of the audience after the details have faded away. The communication tools looked at in Part Four (analogies, examples, demonstrations and stories) are crucial. There is also a brief section on memory in Chapter 5.

2. THE THREE FUNDAMENTALS OF PRESENTATIONS

Fundamental One: Identify the Expert and the Interested Group

There is one very important thing to reflect on before you start. All presentations should involve the communication between an *expert* and an *interested group*. These terms are worth exploring further. Most people reading this book will be reluctant to suggest that they are experts in anything. However, for the purpose of a presentation, you will be the expert, in a particular topic, for a particular audience.

Suppose you have worked on a project for two months and you are asked to make a presentation on the results of this work to the managers of your department. The aim of the presentation is to summarise the outcomes of the project and suggest further action on the basis of these outcomes. The people in the audience are senior managers and have all been in the company longer than you. Not only are they experienced, you can probably assume that they are talented as well. In this situation, it is hard to imagine yourself as the *expert*.

Figure 2.1. Is this a father teaching his child, or is the child showing his father how to use the computer? The term expert is relative, and a presenter will always be the expert in relation to a given audience for a particular presentation task.

However, you are the expert. You are presenting a summary of work that you have carried out. You will talk about what you have done, why you have done it, what the results were and what your recommendations are based on these findings.

On top of this, you can assume the audience is an *interested group*. Fundamentally they have an interest in what you are going to talk about, otherwise, why would they be there? Again, taking the example of the project you have worked on, your boss has delegated a responsibility to you. You have been given a package of work to do and obviously the person who gave you that responsibility will be keen to find out how you got on.

This will always be the case in any presentation that you give, or rather it should always be the case. Sometimes presentations are given out of habit. Companies may organise weekly or monthly briefings without much thought about what specifically they wish to achieve. Always ask yourself the question: 'Am I the best person to be making this presentation, and what are the audience going to get from listening to me?' It acts as a first filter on the whole planning process. Once you can answer this question for yourself, the task will seem far less daunting. You know what you are talking about, and your audience wants to hear you speak. What could be simpler?

Asking this question will also focus your attention on the important aspects of the information that you are going to present.

Let's imagine that you work for an advertising firm, and the two-month project was carried out to research the market for a new product. Let's suppose that your audience is senior managers, all of whom have many years of experience. It helps in this instance to decide what you are the expert in (the results of your two-month study), and this guides you as to what to include in your presentation. If you think like this, you will not waste a lot of time introducing general concepts related to consumer surveys, statistics, and advertising (areas where the real experts are in the audience), and will instead focus on what you have learnt from the work that was carried out.

Fundamental Two: The Aim

'What is the aim of this presentation?' is the first and most important question that you will ask when preparing your material. If you head off in the wrong direction from the start, no amount of excellent visual aids or charismatic delivery is going to turn it around for you. This may

Key point:

Make sure you are the right person to give the presentation (the expert) and that the audience (interested group) has a genuine need that you can satisfy.

sound obvious, but surprisingly often presenters fail to set a realistic aim for their presentations.

When asked about the aim of their presentation most people are able to give a short, concise answer, but very often these answers don't stand up to scrutiny. For example, someone might have given a talk on 'health and safety in the work place'. When asked what the aim of this presentation was, their answer will often be along the lines of: 'I wanted to give an overview of what the key issues are,' or 'I'm responsible for health and safety in our section, and I wanted to summarise the key points for the rest of the staff in this area.' This may sound reasonable, but it's not. It is far too vague and will more than likely result in a bored, inattentive audience and a flat communication.

Often presenters will even add comments like: 'I know it's boring, but it is important that they are made aware of the issues.' This is not a succinct aim for a presentation. Telling a group of people about something because some aspect of this material is important is woolly thinking. This can be demonstrated by a practical example.

Suppose you wished to buy a bicycle to go on short trips at the weekend while at the same time getting some fresh air and exercise. You aren't sure what kind of bike you want for these jaunts or even what kind of bikes are available. You have a rough idea of how much you are prepared to spend, but may bend somewhat on this amount if necessary. You now need to talk to an expert to find out more, so you call in to a cycle shop.

Having introduced yourself and explained your purpose, the shop owner realises that in order to be of assistance to you, he must first arm you with some knowledge. He begins: 'The bicycle, as we know it today, became popular at the end of the 19th Century. Originally the pedals were attached directly to a large front wheel and it was some years before a chain-driven, sprocketed back wheel appeared… There are three main categories of bicycle: touring bikes, racing bikes and mountain bikes… The price of a bicycle is dependent on many things, but in recent years has fallen due to… There are several main manufacturers of bicycles today…' and so on.

This is not a very likely scenario but it follows the same logic as many presentations. In the case of the aforementioned health and safety presentation, the thinking goes: 'This group need to know about health and safety. I am very knowledgeable on health and safety. Therefore, I will summarise the key points of my knowledge in the time that I have to speak.'

In the real world, the bicycle shop owner wouldn't try to communicate in the way described. Certainly he is knowledgeable, and certainly you are in need of knowledge, but a general, encyclopaedic overview on the bicycle is not the way to bridge the gap. Instead, he would quickly try to ascertain what you want (Are you there to browse, to buy, to sell? Are you looking for high performance or just general use?) and he would – from his store of bicycle-related knowledge – present information in order to help you reach your goal of making a decision, and buying a bike.

He would tell you what the main types of bike available are (touring, racing, mountain), what the key features are (gears, comfort, cost, colour) and any other information that may be of use (availability, maintainability, durability and so on). This is no different from a formal presentation. He will use demonstrations, visual aids, examples, even anecdotes to help you make your decision. This presentation had an aim, and now that you are in a position to make a decision, this aim has been achieved.

The same focus can be applied to the health and safety presentation. You have to decide at the start why you are giving the presentation and what you wish to achieve. The 'why' question is vitally important and is very often not asked. So, why is health and safety important? In order to answer the question, you have to look at your audience. Maybe they are new to the company and don't realise how stringent the regulations are. Maybe they have been with the company for a long time but a change in the legislation has rendered certain work practices (like working at heights without a harness) unacceptable. Maybe you are simply worried about a particular health risk. You still haven't got an aim for the presentation, just a reason why a presentation might be necessary.

Let's take the last scenario, where there is a tangible health risk, and let's say that this risk is of hearing impairment due to the installation of a new (and very loud) piece of machinery. It has been decided that the wearing of disposable ear plugs should be mandatory. Now you have an aim. The aim of the presentation is to make everyone aware that they all have to wear ear-plugs in a particular area from now on. They must leave the presentation with this directive firmly planted in their minds.

How you actually achieve this aim is up to you. You may use a case study of somebody who didn't wear ear protection in a similar situation and who suffered severe loss of hearing (this kind of shock therapy is, of course, a favourite on health and safety courses). You may show how employees will get penalised if the regulations are breached. You may

To try:

Write down the aim of a presentation that you are about to give as succinctly as you can. After you have given it, ask as many of your audience to say what they got from listening to the talk. If there is a mismatch between what you intended to do and what they audience perceived you had actually done, ask yourself why. Were your goals clear? Did you spell these goals out for the audience at the start? Did you try to present too much? Did you wrap up your key message in a conclusion? Did you have the right audience to start with?

Never be afraid to ask an audience about a presentation that you have given. You may have to use a bit of tact to get at the real truth but getting honest feedback is the only way that you will improve.

use a stereo to make a comparative demonstration of the difference in noise between the new machine and the old one. In any case, once the aim is clear, ideas for achieving this aim should follow easily.

You should be able to write the aim down in a single sentence. It should be both *tangible* and *realistic*. Looking at *tangible* first, it is often helpful to ask the question: 'What do I want the audience to do as a result of attending my presentation?' or, 'What will they be able to do that they weren't able to before listening to me?' For example, if you are speaking at a political rally, a *tangible* aim would be to get the audience to vote for you, a clear action based on your communication, however, is it *realistic*? This is the second point. Getting people to change their minds, particularly about something that they may feel strongly about, is always extremely difficult. Even if you present a set of water-tight arguments for your candidacy, you will be doing well to convince even a small minority of people in the audience to vote for you on the basis of a single, albeit dazzling, presentation.

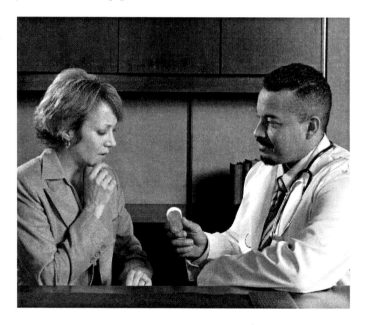

Figure 2.2. A presentation is not just the issuing of information. The presenter should choose, from his or her store of knowledge, a structured package of information that will enable an audience in some way. It should be as focused as a doctor-patient consultation, where only the doctor's knowledge pertaining to the patient's specific needs is presented.

A more realistic aim might be to get the audience to read your manifesto, or to take one away with them. The aim might simply be to provoke the audience to ask questions or to engage in discussion, which might give you a better platform to express yourself. In any case, the aim should be clear to you and the audience and it should be something that it is within your scope to achieve.

It is often difficult to assess whether you have actually managed to meet your presentation targets after the event, but you must set them clearly nonetheless. A presentation with a clear aim has a chance of making an impression on the audience, whereas a presentation without a clear focus can, at the very best, be entertaining and diverting, but is unlikely to remain long in memory.

Fundamental Three: Where Do You Acquire the Skills?

People often say that they would like to learn the 'tips' and 'rules of thumb' to make them into better presenters. This seems natural enough. If you wanted to learn karate you would have to learn the basic moves first, and then you would have to carry out exercises to master these moves in order to perform the art of karate. So it would seem natural to assume that for the art of presenting there must be a set of techniques that need to be mastered. However, the surprising and heartening truth is that there are no such techniques; there are no 'basic moves' for presenting. Or more to the point, you have already mastered these moves and do not need to learn them again.

The reason for this is simple. Presentations and conversations are essentially the same thing. You use the same palette of skills that you have developed through years of conversing with people (and this palette of skills is considerable) as you do when you are making a presentation. Making eye contact; varying your tone, pitch and speed of your voice; injecting energy into your words; telling stories; drawing analogies; using body language to enhance your expression – you have learnt to use all of these techniques and many more to express yourself in conversation, and you can just as effectively use them to express yourself compellingly when making a presentation.

Why then, if it is all so simple, are so many presentations such hard work? Why, for the audience, is it so often hard to follow what the presenter is talking about or to even stay awake? Why do speakers suffer from severe nerves, lose their way, mumble incoherently or go careering over the allotted time without realising it?

Key point:

Write down the aim of your presentation in one sentence.

Figure 2.3. There are no new skills to learn in order to give a presentation. All of the skills necessary are taken from your vast palette of conversational skills, which you go on mastering throughout your life.

The answer lies in the fact that when you converse, you do so without thinking about how you are doing it. You focus on what you're saying and who you're saying it to and take for granted the mechanisms you use to do this – the pauses, the hand gestures, and the changes in tone. However, in the daunting spotlight of the formal presentation (and make no mistake, it is daunting for everyone who has to do it), you become overly self-aware and start trying to consciously control the mechanisms of communication. But these mechanisms are innate, and therein lies the solution. If you can plan the presentation in such a way as to allow yourself to 'be yourself', you can present with all the energy and fluency with which you chat to a friend.

Quite often people deliberately spurn their conversational skill-set in an effort to present in a formal manner. Take, for example, a presentation given by the manager of a small accounting firm. The speaker, with many years of business and presenting experience, gave a very professional talk, looked at everyone in his audience, spoke clearly and kept to time. It was all very composed, but there was something missing. The presenter seemed distant and lifeless, he seemed to be in what can be called the 'glass box' of presenting. He was visibly there, but somehow removed at the same time.

On video the speaker could see a marked difference between his style during the talk and the questions afterwards. During the talk he was inhibited and severe, the information was listed and flat, and his delivery was monotonic and unbroken. However, for the questions (during which the speaker was more obviously conversing with, rather than speaking at, the audience) he was relaxed, friendly, open and enthused.

Why the difference? The manager said that he had felt more relaxed while taking questions but for the main part of the talk had deliberately affected a more serious style. 'I thought that this was more appropriate for a formal presentation,' he suggested.

The term 'formal presentation' sounds a danger bell. If a presentation were described as 'important' or 'crucial', for example, that would indicate how much is riding on the presentation for the audience. But the term 'formal' can suggest that the presenter should not only take his task seriously, but somehow change his personal style to reflect this, and this is never helpful.

Certainly, during an important presentation you might decide not to tell a joke or use a particular story, but that does not mean that you need to become a different person. If someone stops you in the corridor in work and asks you what time it is, you will most likely look them in the eye and tell them the time. Likewise, if you are asked a question during or after a presentation, you look at the audience and give them an answer. So it is with all presenting: look the audience in the eye and tell them what you know. With a bit of practice, you can present as fluidly and naturally as you speak. Your conversational instincts, subtle and powerful, will then be allowed to take full flight.

Key point:

Use your normal conversational skills when presenting.

13

PART TWO: PREPARATION

This part of the book looks at what goes on before the presentation. This preparation phase is a two-fold process. Firstly, it is concerned with choosing and organising material so that it is interesting, clear and memorable. Secondly, it is a quality assurance process for the talk you are about to give. Any of the things that can go wrong when delivering a presentation (losing your way, running out of time, equipment failing, losing the attention of the audience) can be eliminated at this stage with excellent preparation. And there is no short-cut for this. Good presentations always look effortless, but this is only because the speaker has prepared well in order to keep everything under control.

These chapters on preparation are laid out chronologically. In other words, they form a suggested sequence of steps that will bring your material together. So, it is worth pointing out straight away that the chapter on visual aids comes right at the end. Many people start with the visual aids and then think about what they wish to say about each one, which is totally wrong. One of the main reasons for this is the over-emphasis placed on PowerPoint. In fact many people see a presentation simply as a PowerPoint file. A presentation, however, is a live event, a communication from a person to a group. The decisions on what you are going to say, and in what order, should be made first, and only then can you turn your attention to visual aids.

The steps for preparation are laid out in the following order, and there is a chapter dedicated to each.

1. Decide on scope
2. Brainstorm topic
3. Structure material – introduction and conclusion
4. Prepare guide notes
5. Prepare visual aids

Preparation is a decision-making process. By the end of this section, you will be able to work through this process to produce a sensibly structured presentation. All of this presupposes that you have first outlined a clear aim for yourself, as discussed in Chapter 2. It is worth stressing again that if you have not got a clear and realistic plan of what you wish to achieve, then you are doomed from the start. If you have, then you are ready to start generating and ordering your ideas.

3. SCOPE

The first thing to do is to mark out the patch from which you will mine your material. The scope of your presentation is set by three things: topic, audience, and time. These items form three boundaries that mark out the territory of your material. Some people might suggest the venue as being another important factor. But this is only a cosmetic consideration, affecting, say, how you might present your visual material, or whether you need a microphone. It will not alter what you wish to say.

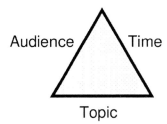

Figure 3.1. *The topic you are going to speak on, the audience you are going to speak to, and the time you have to speak form three boundaries that limit the amount of material you can include.*

When you were deciding on the aim of the talk, you would have already considered each of these items. It is important not to stray outside the boundaries that you have set. Straying off the *topic*, for example, may seem like a reasonable and interesting digression for you, but for the audience it may be hugely confusing. Remember, they are hearing this for the first time and will assume that everything is relevant. The speaker wandering off the point would be like a director putting a scene into a film with no relation to the overall plot. The audience would watch the scene and wonder, 'Why are we seeing this? What's going on here?' only to be disappointed or confused at a later stage. The same is true in a presentation. The audience implicitly assumes that everything that they see is part of the plot, so you have to be aware of where you are going at all times and stick to your task.

It is also important to have a clear sight of who your *audience* is. People often ask what they should do if there is a big split in the audience. For example, there may be technical people and sales people in the same group who will have very different levels of understanding. There

Many people define the aims of their presentation in terms of what they are going to 'cover'. This is utterly wrong. The only way the presentation should be judged is in terms of what the audience has actually understood. However, even this is a little vague. A more concrete measure of achievement is to say what the audience is now able to do that they weren't able to do before the talk.

When setting out the aims of your presentation, define them in terms of what it is that you wish the audience to be able to do as a result of listening to you, e.g. make a decision, start an informed discussion, use a computer system, or go about getting further instruction on how to use a computer system. This will force you to be more audience-focused and to set more realistic aims for your presentations.

is, however, no solution to this problem. If you are trying to pitch to two different audiences the situation is fundamentally flawed. This would be like two patients going to see a doctor together. Unless they have very similar conditions, there is no way that the words of that doctor could be of relevance to both people at the same time. It is vital that you know your audience and that you only try to communicate material that fulfils a need of the whole audience.

The last item to be mindful of is *time*. Simply put, you must stick to time. Always. The audience is listening to new material and listening is hard work. If you say at the outset how long you intend to speak for (and you should), the audience will prepare themselves to listen for that time. If you then exceed this, you will be breaking a promise and this can make people very resentful. They will not express this disaffection; they will most probably just sit quietly and listen, with maybe the odd glance at a watch as you whitter on, but it is precisely this lack of expression that drives their frustration. They are at your mercy and when you start to exceed the allotted time, an intense frustration sets in as they wonder: 'Will this ever end?'

Everyone has experienced the tedium of an ultra-long presentations. There is no excuse for this and you will undermine any good work that you have done as soon as you start to overshoot the allotted time. Sometimes presenters say that they can't possibly squeeze all of their material into a short space of time but this is absurd. If you are asked to speak for five minutes, implicit in this is a request for how much depth you should go into.

In some situations, presenters stick to their time but rush through their material to make it fit. This is another version of the same problem, and will only exhaust the audience. If you have so much to say that you have to rush, then say less and take your time.

One grey area associated with timing arises when the audience asks questions during the presentation. This will obviously slow you down but it is no bad thing. If the audience is asking questions this is always preferable to the situation where you are doing all of the talking. Factor in some time to allow for this, and if things get out of hand, politely suggest that a proper discussion wait until the end of the talk.

In some smaller group situations, particularly with a group that know each other, presentations can turn into meetings where the formal presentation almost becomes secondary. In this case, you may well run over time but it doesn't matter so much because if everyone is involved,

3. Scope

then it is no longer a pure listening exercise and the participants are unlikely to be bored. It is hard to be bored when you're talking yourself. Just remember, though, that you are still the host for the proceedings and it's your responsibility to keep things moving along.

Finally, the question is often asked, 'How long should I speak for?' This is obviously dependent on subject matter, speaker and audience but a generally accepted figure for how long people can listen, before attention starts to flag, even in an engaging talk, is about 20 minutes. Interestingly, most college lectures run for more than twice this time, and yet few lecturers take a break in the middle of their lectures.

The 20-minute rule is not so sacrosanct when the audience is involved in the presentation – asking questions or engaging in activities – but it is always worth bearing it in mind. And if you finish before the allotted time, very few people will mind.

Key point:

Set three limits for your material based on the topic, the audience and the time you have to speak.

4. BRAINSTORMING

Now that you have the aim and the scope of the talk clearly defined, you must decide how you are going to achieve this aim. There are many different ways to approach this task, and this chapter looks at how to generate these ideas.

Let's say that you work for a company that makes something – anything – it could be cars; it could be cardboard boxes; it doesn't matter. You are in charge of one of the production lines in the factory, but you have become concerned about the reliability of one of the processes. This is an important process and is carried out by a new machine. The factory is under pressure to reach an end-of-year target so this machine is working at full capacity. You have noticed that there has been an increase in the number of defective parts produced. You would like to investigate further but know that this won't sit well with your boss, as it will result in downtime. However, your instincts tell you that the defects being produced could point to a serious fault, which if left unchecked could lead to far greater problems in the long run.

You are due to make a presentation to senior managers (including your boss) about the current status of this process. You are going to take the opportunity to lobby for a complete line shut-down to check the fault. There are many ways you could set about trying to communicate this message. Here, for example, are six different approaches:

- Work out the cost associated with stopping the line for different numbers of days and plot these on a bar chart. On the same chart plot, in a different colour, the expense that you estimate could be accrued if this problem were left unchecked. The aim here is to highlight the difference, in scale, between the short-term penalty and the long-term one.
- Cite a report on a machine failure that led to a serious accident in the past. Show that some of the defects being produced by this new machine are similar to those experienced prior to that accident.
- Present the findings of a straw poll among the technicians who work on that line, showing that eight out of nine of them would prefer to shut down production to inspect the new machine.
- Present a simple analysis that shows how long a line shut-down could be tolerated if the end-of-year target were still to be met and request two-thirds of this time to inspect the machine.

4. Brainstorming

- Remind the audience of the story of the Challenger space shuttle disaster, where an eagerness to meet launch targets for the year resulted in safety concerns being expediently ignored, with tragic consequences.
- Remind the audience of your excellent employment record with the company, and cite some statistics showing how infrequently your product line has been shut down. Then use this to lever the argument that you would normally not be so conservative, but that you are particularly concerned this time around.

You could take any of these very different approaches, or any number of other approaches, or a combination of several. The point you are trying to make is the same in each case, but there are literally hundreds of ways you can go about making this point. However, most people dive straight into writing up a set of bullet points, possibly including a few pictures or graphs, and then they stand up and speak this through. In doing so, they are eliminating the majority of the really good presentation approaches they could adopt.

To try:

At no point is the input of others more useful to you than at the brainstorming stage. Get a small group of friends or colleagues together. Tell them what the talk is about, to whom it will be given and for how long, and let the ideas flow. Do not reject or criticise suggestions in the early stages, just write everything down. Then discuss the ideas generated and make a selection of what you think are the best ones. Conclude the session by writing this up into a rough plan. At this stage leave the material for a few days (if time permits) as this incubation period will allow other connected ideas to surface. Only then should you start the formal preparation process.

A brainstorming session like this may take as little as five or ten minutes, and it is guaranteed to generate several ideas that you would never have come up with on your own.

Figure 4.1. There are literally thousands of ways you can approach a presentation task. Really original ideas can only be born if you take time to entertain many possibilities at the brainstorming phase. How else would someone have thought of using a toucan to advertise Guinness Stout?

It is really useful to engage in some kind of brainstorming before you prepare any presentation. This works best if you can get other people to help you, but even doing it on your own will pay dividends.

Brainstorming not only helps you to generate ideas, but also to make a final selection and order these ideas. By writing all of your brainstormed ideas down, you are in a better position to choose which items to include or omit, and then to order those that you have chosen. A good approach for a longer presentation is to write all of the possible items for the talk – points, pictures, stories, graphs, demonstrations, exercises – on separate pieces of card and lay them out on the table in front of you. It is like laying all of the pieces of a puzzle on the table, or all of the components of something you are trying to assemble on the floor, before you start. It effectively increases the capacity of your short-term working memory, which is normally very limited, as will be discussed in Chapter 13.

5. STRUCTURE

This is an extremely important chapter. Now that you have outlined a clear aim for your talk, and you have decided what material you will include, how should you put it together so that it delivers your argument effectively and memorably? The answer is one of the most well-trodden axioms of presentations, and it can be stated as follows:

- Say what you're going to say.
- Say it.
- Say what you have just said.

This may not earth-shattering to some of you. To others it will appear positively staid and dreary, but it contains a truism that is profoundly important to all presentations. The above advice could be phrased in a different way. For everything that you wish to present, you must include some kind of an introduction and some kind of a conclusion to make the presentation truly effective.

The role of the introduction is to set a context for what is about to come. It puts the audience in the picture. It gives them a clear idea of where they will be going and why.

The role of the conclusion is different. As the last thing that you say, the conclusion will be the most memorable. It thus acts as the final and most important message of your talk. It reminds the audience of where you have brought them. This should line up exactly with the aim. Once you have decided on the aim of your talk, you have, effectively, written your conclusion.

These two components appear in all functional communications, and this can be clearly illustrated by means of an everyday example. Let's say you are at work and you phone home to talk to your husband and you begin with the following statement:

'Hi, it's me. I'm ringing about this party tonight. I need you to do something for me.'

In four seconds you've completed your introduction. You have set a context for the conversation and given an idea of what you will be communicating and why. The context you have set is that you need something, and there is more information to follow. If you opened with:

'Hi, it's me. How're things?'

Then you would have set a very different context. You would have been implying that you were simply ringing for a chat. Because you know the person well, setting the context is very easy and you do not have to do a lot of pre-explaining. How you set a context will always depend on what the audience knows from before. Now that the introduction is finished, you can proceed. You say:

> 'I'm held up in work. The stuff we are doing will probably run on until after six but not much later. I'll be able to go to the party but I won't have time to go home first. So I'll meet you there, but I left the present in the locker beside my bed. Can you bring it?'

This is the main body of the presentation: the 'who, what, when, where, why'. You have now told the full story and the person at the other end doesn't seem to have any burning questions. So, you're about to sign off, but before you do, you say one last thing. Can you imagine what this is? Well, a plausible suggestion might be:

> 'So, whatever you do, don't forget the present.'

This, in fairness, is the only reason that you rang. You knew that you wouldn't have time to go home, you wouldn't be able to collect the present and you wanted your husband to do this for you. So this is where you place your final emphasis and it becomes the conclusion of the communication. It's the point you wish to drive home. The same scenario might have a different conclusion. You may just be ringing to say that you will go straight to the party and that your husband shouldn't wait for you to come home, in which case your parting message might be:

> 'So, don't wait for me, I'll meet you at the party.'

Here you're imparting a different message but whatever the message is, it should be spelt out by the conclusion.

Although the conclusion is what you want the audience to go away with, you can not just state this conclusion and hope that they will accept the bare truth of what you are saying. You need to convince them, and to do this you need to take them through various arguments and explanations in order to build a platform on which your conclusion can logically sit. Again, looking at the example of the phone conversation, you could just pick up the phone and cut to the chase by saying something like:

> 'Hi. It's me. Bring the present in my locker to the party.'

This, apart from being very rude, would be a conclusion without justification and the person at the receiving end would be left with more questions than answers. What present? Why can't you bring it? Where will you be? And so on.

The body of the presentation brings the audience to a conclusion. But rather than leaving them to decide what this conclusion is for themselves, it makes sense to spell it out. You will also have told them to expect this conclusion during the introduction. If the audience doesn't know where you are going to take them, then they will not realise it is worth their while to listen. Also, if they don't know where they are going, they won't know what to listen out for and how to make sense of the pieces of information that you are delivering. This vital component – setting a context by means of the introduction – will be the focus in the next section.

Figure 5.1. Even a telephone conversation – one that has a purpose – will be structured with an introduction and a conclusion.

The Introduction – Setting a Context

Trying to decipher a piece of text in a foreign language is a lot like listening to some presentations, namely presentations where a context has not been set at the start. When you read foreign prose, you constantly ask, 'What is this about?' If you can crack this, if you can get the gist of the piece, then you can second-guess what a lot of the individual sentences mean. You might not understand every word, but from a general understanding of what the piece is about, you can guess what the words probably mean.

In a presentation, if you know from the start where the presenter intends to take you and why, then it is easy to see where each point, each story and diagram fit into the overall journey. If you are not sure where you are going, then the presentation is just a jumble of ideas and they are harder to understand because of this. Very often presenters rush through the introduction so that they can get stuck into their material. But this is very foolish, and is symptomatic of a presentation without a clear aim.

It's a bit like doing a jig-saw puzzle without the picture. You could follow instructions of where to place each piece (like the old paint-by-numbers sets) but the process won't have much meaning for you until the picture is nearly complete. However, if you know what the picture is supposed to look like from the start, you can get more meaning from the exercise. It is vital to paint this overview picture at the outset, but this is not always so easily done, as will now be explored.

Listed introductions – Most people have the sense to use some kind of introduction in their presentation but it is worth looking closely at what these introductions actually achieve. In order to examine this, it may help to look at the following two introductory slides taken from conference presentations on totally different topics. They are shown side by side in Figure 5.2.

Introduction 1	Introduction 2
• Background to Project	• Introduction
• Objectives	• Work Done so Far
• Work Accomplished	• Future Work
• Work Remaining	• Conclusions

Figure 5.2. Two introduction slides taken from two technical presentations. Although clear, neither actually tells the audience anything about what they can expect from the presentation. The interchangeability of the two slides indicates that neither is likely to be very descriptive about that particular presentation.

These were the exact words used, and you may be thinking that they are fairly clear and reasonable. And so they are, but what do they tell the audience? In what way are the audience prepared for the ensuing presentation?

Suppose you went into a travel agent and you told him that you were in desperate need of a break. 'Of course,' beams the travel agent, 'We have just the thing for you.' He explains, 'We have a truly fantastic one-week holiday deal. You will fly to a foreign destination where the weather will be clement and the local culture will be engagingly different from what you are used to. You will reside in some kind of paid lodging and will socialise with various people. You will eat the local food and probably go out and engage in evening entertainments. At the end of the week, you will experience a feeling of well-being and will travel home refreshed and happy.'

Would you book this holiday? If you really felt like a mystery tour you might, but if, like most people, you would like to know what to expect before making a decision, you would need to know more. Certainly all of the things described will happen – the change in climate, the socialising, the different cuisine – but these things happen on most holidays. The information that you have been given doesn't discriminate this holiday from any other.

This is also true of the introductions pictured in Figure 5.2. Certainly there will be a section on background and on conclusions, but aren't there always? The two introductions are side by side to show how interchangeable they are. And remember they are taken from two totally different presentations. They are like the description of the holiday – they tell you what will happen, but nothing useful. An introduction like those shown is not far removed from saying, 'I will speak; you will listen; I will finish; you will ask some questions; we will all go home.'

Going back to the travel agent, a more useful and engaging introduction might be as follows: 'How would you fancy going on safari? You'll be exploring the African plains, sleeping under canvas, following elephants across the savannah, watching spectacular sunsets at dusk.' This paints a mental picture and immediately you can imagine yourself there. The reason that this works is that it draws on a specific memory reference rather than a general, abstract one. Your experience and knowledge of the world can help the travel agent to paint his picture, so much so in this case that even the single word 'safari' would probably trigger off a clear enough idea of what was going to follow.

Certainly this is not enough. You would then wish to know a lot more: the cost, the type of accommodation, who you will be with, what specific activities you will engage in and so on, but this is still only the introduction stage, and in setting a context and giving you an overview of what will be involved, it has been useful.

In most work presentations you aren't looking to conjure up evocative mental imagery in this way, but the same principle applies. Describing what the presentation will be about in general, abstract terms is of little use. It is far more effective to set a context using real ideas that the audience can relate to. The use of tangible rather than abstract ideas will be explored in detail in Part Four, but for now it may help to show how this can be applied to the introduction by referring to a specific example.

A colleague once asked for some advice on a presentation that he was to give in the area of 'rapid prototyping'. The presentation was about 25 minutes long and he asked if he could do a dry run and get some feedback. The presenter's style, the visual aids and the various other communication tools used during the presentation were all very engaging and the presenter in question was extremely good, but at the end of the talk the point of the whole thing was still unclear. The reason for this lack of coherence was simply a lack of introduction.

The speaker had shown an introductory slide but it didn't set any context. After some discussion, he tried a new approach. He began by introducing himself and without showing any slides or lists or plans for the talk, he walked right up to the audience with a computer mouse in his hand. He asked how much they thought the plastic casing of this device would cost. People made several guesses, he told them the answer and, as you can imagine for such a mass-produced item, it wasn't very much. Then he followed with another question, 'How much do think the metal mould used to make this part would cost?' Again, after several guesses, he gave the answer, only this time the figure was astronomically large, of the order of tens of thousands of euro.

He then used this to lever his critical point, that the mould is a complex three-dimensional object with very high design and development costs, so any mistakes in its design could prove very costly. Wouldn't it be very useful, then, he argued, to be able to make such a mould quickly, with a cheap and flexible material, and then test it thoroughly, without the huge cost associated with the final metal prototype? This kind of design troubleshooting is called 'rapid prototyping'.

By doing this, he was leading the audience into his talk in a relaxed way and at the same time setting a context for everything that would follow. It was now clear, through a simple practical example, why you would wish to do this and the presentation that followed would make more sense against this backdrop.

Whatever the presentation and whatever the aim, take your time with the introduction. If you are in too much of a hurry to get going, you may lose everyone just minutes after you start to speak and everything else that you say will be worthless. An example introduction may help to show how context can be set at the start that will help the audience to make sense of what you say.

Example introduction: 'Any questions?' – You work for a company that develops computer software. You are in charge of a dedicated team of software engineers who develop the products as well as the user manuals that go with them. However, following a recent product launch, your sales team has reported that users have found the new software difficult to use, and poorly supported by the manual.

You decide that the best way to sort this problem out would be to gather the entire sales team together and make a presentation of what the new product does and how to use it. However, this is not just a presentation to a passive audience. The aim is to identify the shortcomings, from a user perspective, in the software and in the associated user manual.

So, in the introduction you do the following. You ask all of the sales team to take out a pen and sheet of paper. You say that you will go through the main points, with whatever accompanying demonstrations are necessary, and you want each member of the team to make a note of anything that is confusing or improperly explained. You will then chair a question-and-answer session before finally asking one of the team to write a report summarising the most important matters that were raised in this discussion.

This instruction sets a very clear context for the audience. They are to see themselves as *inspectors* for the presentation. The items that they fail to understand are to be noted and discussed, not, as is usually the case when an audience is baffled, just forgotten about. They have a clear instruction as to what they should do with the presented material, and this makes them more responsive.

Had you not given this instruction, they might have become bored by the catalogue of material that you presented, and disillusioned by the fact that there was much of it that they did not understand. If you then asked which bits they had the most difficulty with at the end, they wouldn't be prepared for this question and would not be able to engage in the discussion you had planned.

Figure 5.3. Context enables people to make sense of the details of your talk. Above are images from Crooks in the Cloisters *and* Psycho. *Without any knowledge of these films, it would not be obvious that the first is a daft comedy and the second a tense thriller. With this context set, the viewer will interpret each very differently.*

In general, presenters tend to under-introduce their material and this greatly undermines the ensuing communication. Take your time with the introduction. Think about where you are going to take your audience and then be kind enough to share this vision with them.

Selling the Presentation

The discussion so far has really been about *where* a presentation should go but not so much about *why*. The task of setting out a realistic and useful aim was explored in Chapter 4, but telling the audience where you are going to go is not quite enough, you must also tell them why they should want to go there. You must answer the question that will be on everyone's lips: 'What's in this for me?'

This may sound like a callous appraisal of the average presentation audience but it reflects a general truism of human nature: people always have a reason for doing things, you can always say why you did something. These reasons need not be strictly selfish, but they will still be reasons. A person may run for many reasons: to catch a bus, to get fit, for pleasure, to raise money for charity, to escape a fire. But a person walking casually down a street will not suddenly break into a sprint for no reason at all.

5. Structure

If you want to get your audience's attention, you need to tell them at the outset why they should listen to your talk. You need to motivate them to pay attention. Gimmicks are not the best way, because although telling a joke or getting everyone to walk around the room will break the ice, it doesn't sell the content of the presentation. However, there are many ways to both get attention and to sell your presentation. They can also contribute to your introduction in helping to set the context. Some suggestions are as follows:

- A story
- An interesting or remarkable fact
- A quotation
- A question to the audience
- An engaging picture
- A demonstration

These tools not only get the audience focused, but the presenter too. The start is always the most nervous time for the presenter, and if you have something concrete to start off with, it gets you through that first awkward minutes of speaking.

A story – Stories work on two levels. Firstly, they personalise your presentation, making it more engaging to the audience. Secondly, they are a memory packaging tool for past experiences that mankind has been using for thousands of years. They therefore usually form a stronger memory in the mind of the audience than a lot of disparate facts.

The CEO of an electronics company uses this technique frequently, often referring at the start of presentations to the fact that the firm started trading in 1999 and survived the subsequent sharp decline in the technology sector. He sometimes uses the phrase 'we have walked through the desert' to describe how the company has survived the worst recession in the technology sector in thirty years. He is not afraid to take his time when telling this story.

In doing this he uses story on the two levels mentioned above. Firstly, he gets people's attention and personalises the company in a way that makes them stand out in the memory of the audience. Secondly, he lays down the main theme for the presentation, namely that the company should be credible in the eyes of the audience, who are potential customers. Establishing credibility is really the central theme of any sales presentation. If the company have survived such a recession whilst in the tricky start-up phase, then they must be doing something right. Throughout the rest of the talk he can build on this theme, using examples and case studies to bear each point out, but for now, he has got people's attention and given them a good reason to continue to pay attention.

An interesting or remarkable fact – A speaker once began his talk on energy conservation with a brief account of his recent trip to a conference in Hong Kong, after which he was horrified to calculate that 440 kg of aviation fuel had been used to get him there and back. This amount of fuel (about six times his own body weight) is equivalent to what many motorists use in a year.

The effect here is to immediately grab attention, and to act as a seed thought for the presentation: 'Can we continue to undervalue our diminishing stocks of fossil fuels?' What the presenter then wants the audience to do (ask a question, sign a petition, lobby parliament, start a riot) is another matter, which must then be spelt out, but the dual goals of getting attention and setting context have been achieved.

A quotation – A good quotation is like a good photograph. It both expresses some wise truism or insight (like a photograph, you can see this straight away) and it does this concisely and eloquently (also like a photograph, the composition, colour and focus are clear). It grabs attention, and if wisely chosen, can also establish one of your main themes.

Figure 5.4. A quotation not only borrows an eloquent insight, but also aligns you with great and famous people.

It doesn't have to be from somebody famous either, just someone relevant to your audience. However, it should be someone who is respected by the audience. In this way, you are aligning yourself with someone highly regarded, which will add credence to your words. For this reason, a lot of the great people of history have had their eloquent reflections appropriated for presentations the world over.

At a talk on innovation management, the main theme of which was that it is not breakthroughs in technology that drive progress in a company, but rather how the people within the organisation react to and manage these new technologies, who better to cite than the most famous scientist of all – Albert Einstein:

> 'The release of atomic energy has not created a new problem. It has merely made more urgent the necessity of solving an existing one.'

In other words, how we use technology is up to us; the technology itself is not to blame.

Einstein wasn't the only heavyweight to contribute to this particular talk. At a later stage, on the subject of fearlessly embracing new technology, Henry Ford was enlisted:

> 'I am looking for a lot of men who have an infinite capacity to not know what can't be done.'

In fact, very often the themes of technical presentations can be quite general. Presentations don't lend themselves to the communication of detail. Also, the biggest factors in any technical field are the people who use this technology and the human skills they bring to bear. So quotations can come from very far outside of the immediate technical domain. Winston Churchill's words were used in a talk on the need for creativity and innovation in a particular research sector, with the words:

> 'Success is the ability to go from one failure to another with no loss of enthusiasm.'

Sir Winston also had the last word, as the presentation finished emphatically with:

> 'History will be kind to me, for I intend to write it.'

A question to the audience – Any kind of audience interaction is good for a presentation. It's hard for an audience to be bored if they are actively involved. Even if the audience is not required to answer a question out loud, just asking one will make them more receptive to your ensuing material, and will motivate them to keep listening.

Consider the following example, from a presentation on the topic of quality control. The presenter asked the audience how many people would have to be in a room to get an odds-on chance of finding two people with the same birthday. She then asked for suggestions to be called out and came up with an average answer from the audience based on several shows of hands.

The actual number of people you would have to gather to get a better-than-evens chance of finding two with the same birthday is only 23. This is a lot lower than most people guess, and was well below the figure agreed on by the audience, which was around 180. The reason is that although the number of different birthdays is 365, if you work out all of the possible permutations of matches between as few as 23 people, you get enough to give you just greater than a 50% chance of finding two with the same birthday.

She then went on to demonstrate this surprising statistic. There were about 60 people in the room for this presentation and this gives a 99.3% chance of finding a match. So she passed around a calendar and asked each person in turn to circle their birthday, and when the first person encountered a match, they were to raise their hand. This happened after only 18 people had marked the calendar, and by the end of the exercise, she had found no fewer than four matches in the audience.

Why did she do this? This talk was on quality control and statistical methods for keeping industrial processes stable. The concept behind this is a complicated one, but the key point that she wanted to make was that without the use of statistical tools, human beings are very poor at intuitively reasoning about probabilities, which was borne out by the inaccurate answers given. By using this exercise, she not only aroused the audience's curiosity and got them actively involved from the start, but she also demonstrated clearly the main point of her talk.

A potential complication has probably jumped into the mind of some readers. With 60 people in the room, she was 99.3% sure of finding two people with the same birthday, but what if this group fell into the 0.7% for whom there was no match? This raises another point about putting questions to the audience, which is that, like a good lawyer, you should never ask a question for which you don't know the answer. She was, indeed, taking a slight risk, but you should never be afraid to do this. The discussion that would ensue in the event of finding no match would still make for a more engaging presentation than a simple one-sided discourse on the part of the presenter.

It would, of course, be worth planning what you might say in this eventuality. One back-up plan would be to repeat the exercise but this time ask each member of the audience to circle their mother's birth date.

An engaging picture – Everyone loves to look at pictures. Having a picture at the start of a presentation will capture people's attention and more easily lodge an idea into their memory. It can also be chosen to exemplify one of the main themes of your talk.

There was a television programme made several years ago for the Open University on the topic of engineering failure. The main theme of the programme was how risks are assessed on large engineering projects. Not surprisingly, the most spectacular and engaging examples were used as case studies. The opening titles showed footage of the Challenger space shuttle disaster in 1986. A presentation on any number of similar topics ('The history of space travel', 'The future of space travel', 'Engineering ethics', 'The media and science', 'Science and risk') could fruitfully have used the same example.

To try:

For a presentation that you are about to give, think of at least five different possible introductions. It will again be easier to do this with the help of one or more colleagues. Be divergent in your thinking. Consider the audience and try to bridge from something that is relevant to them to the main content of the talk.

Figure 5.5. An engaging picture or example is a good way to hook audiences at the start of a presentation. Pictures of September Eleventh, for example, will remain shocking and engaging for many years. Think of the many presentation topics that could logically use this example as an opening.

A demonstration – Showing is more effective than telling. It is an altogether more tangible experience than just hearing someone's words. Take this presentation on a new plug-in data acquisition device, for example.

'Data acquisition' means using a computer to automatically take measurements. Traditionally, to get a computer to do this, you needed to install a special plug-in card into your computer, which was time-consuming, difficult and expensive. It was something that usually involved a steep learning curve. But the new devices that were being presented plugged into the USB port on your computer and allowed even an uninitiated user, to be tooled up in no time.

The key point was that these new devices were quick and easy to use. So, he started a stopwatch and then proceeded to take one such device out of the box and install it into his laptop. He showed how the computer detected and installed the new hardware automatically by projecting the display of the laptop onto a large screen. Within a couple of minutes he had a functioning data acquisition device, which was ready to use. He had successfully made his main point – the ease of use – and had motivated the audience to listen to the other points he wished to make about the product. The lack of polish on the whole activity – the fact that he was literally pulling the wires and connectors out of the box for the first time – only added to the attention-grabbing theatre of this introduction.

The Conclusion

What has to be done at the end of a presentation to wrap everything up? The answer to this question is: very little. The work on the conclusion has already been done, and it was done when the aims for the presentation were set out. When you have set out a clear target for where you want to take the audience, you have already written your conclusion.

Another way of saying this is that, although the conclusion comes at the end of the presentation, it is actually the first thing you write. You start by deciding where you want to the audience to go, and then you work out how you are going to get them there. This sounds obvious, but it is frequently not the approach adopted. Conclusions are often just a list of points that recap the main sections of the presentation, with no conclusion having been reached.

As the last thing that the audience hears, the conclusion will be the most memorable. This gives you the platform to really drive home your key point or points. If there has been any doubt, you can tie up the loose ends by spelling out the conclusion you want the audience to reach. Remember, you are the expert, and it is your job to draw conclusions from the mass of material that the audience is not expert enough to decipher and navigate for themselves.

It is again helpful to think of what you want the audience to do. So, if you are speaking at a union meeting, the aim of your talk may simply be to gauge the mood of the workforce in order that you can report this back to senior management. You may talk about several different issues during the presentation; you may show graphs that report on how the company is doing in the marketplace; you may answer questions and chair debate; but at the end of all of this, you would like to poll the assembled audience on how they feel about what they have heard.

Your conclusion, therefore, is to stress the importance of the activity, and to use this to persuade the audience to fill in the questionnaires they have been given. You must impress on the audience the importance of making their feelings known to management, which they can only do by handing in these forms. This is, after all you have said, what you want them to do. This, therefore, is the conclusion.

What Will Be Remembered?

Think about a presentation you have been to, a good one – one that made an impression on you. Now, write down everything that you can remember from that presentation. It's probably not very much and that the things you do remember are probably general insights rather than individual facts. You might remember a story that the presenter told, or an interesting exercise or demonstration or an eye-catching picture. And you might remember one or two compelling truisms from everything that was said. But it's most likely not a huge amount, nor is it very specific.

A doctor recently attended some evening talks on continuing professional development. One such presentation was on heart disease. The talk aimed to educate doctors on new developments in the area that could be of use to them when seeing patients. It lasted for just under two hours but there was a break in the middle and some time to ask questions at the end. The audience got a copy of the presentation slides as part of a set of handouts, and there were a total of 92 slides in all.

Afterwards the doctor said that the presentation had been fairly good, that the presenter had had a very engaging style, and that it was interesting if a little long. But, when asked what she remembered, she could only name two things, along the lines of, 'I learned about the importance of…' or, 'I realised that heart disease differed from other illnesses in regard to…'

The 92 slides, many of which contained bullet points, yielded 331 separate points of information, not to mention three information-rich graphs. All of these pieces of data had left just two insights in the mind of a well-motivated member of the audience.

A technical presentation should, of course, contain facts and figures – just because something isn't remembered explicitly doesn't mean that it does no useful work. Facts, figures, graphs and statistics all act as evidence for the arguments that you make. They serve to bear out what you are saying. But the important point to keep in mind is that, although the details reinforce the general point of your talk, it will be the general point (if anything) that is remembered, not the details.

Take the following three sentences. Which of them do you remember reading in the last few minutes:

'The conclusion of the presentation and the aim of the presentation are effectively the same thing.'

'When you have set out a clear target for where you want to take the audience, you have already written your conclusion.'

'The aim of the presentation at the start will not be the same as the conclusion that you reach at the end.'

You probably had little trouble eliminating the third sentence. However, it's not as easy to choose between the first two. They say essentially the same thing, but with different words in a different order. We quickly forget this word-by-word detail and instead remember the more general meaning extracted from these words. In fact the second sentence is the one taken verbatim from the previous text.

This process of extracting the gist of information and forgetting the details happens all the time. When you read a book, you may turn a page every couple of minutes. Every page brings 30 or 40 new lines of text, as many as 400 new words, upwards of 50 or 60 punctuation marks, not to mention other defining features such as paragraph and chapter breaks. All of this information, and two minutes later a brand new batch, just as rich in detail. People often sit and read for hours, absorbing literally tens of thousands of discrete pieces of information at a time. To remember all of this would involve a phenomenal effort of memory so we don't, we remember the gist: the plot, impressions of the characters, the mood, the tone of the narrator, perhaps even some notion of satire or irony between the lines depending on our level of insight. We literally summarise as we read. We take in the details, extract meaning from them and then throw these details away.

5. Structure

There is no student who has not wished at one time or another to have a photographic memory. And yet, a perfect information storage system of this sort would be weak in precisely the way the human memory is most powerful. The cognitive psychology literature abounds with studies on memory but from all of this, two simple insights are useful for us to consider here:

1. Memory is quite inaccurate, much more than people realise.
2. It is this inaccuracy that makes memory truly powerful.

These two statements are tied up in what it means to be an expert. Experts have the ability to see the wood from the trees. They are able to see the general patterns and truisms in a field of knowledge instead of being overwhelmed by the details. There are many examples of this but one interesting case was displayed by a study carried out on expert chess players.

For this experiment, chess pieces were placed randomly on a board. It is important to note that the pieces were not restricted to certain positions as they would be in an actual game but were just scattered anywhere. The board was shown to a group of expert chess players and to a group of non chess players for a brief period. The two groups were then asked to write down the positions of as many pieces as they could remember. It might be supposed that the chess players would perform better at this memory task than the non-players but this was not the case. Both groups performed equally well (or equally badly, it may be truer to say) remembering only the positions of about four pieces on average.

The test was then repeated, except that this time the pieces were arrayed in a plausible game scenario. The memory task was repeated, and as before, the novices could only remember the position of a few pieces. However, the performance of the expert chess players improved dramatically. They were now able to remember the positions of nearly all 25 pieces on the board, even when they weren't told in advance that their memories would be tested.

Why? Well, with the pieces in a realistic game scenario, the experts were able to perceive a pattern, which they then remembered. By recalling this pattern, they were able to re-construct the positions of a great many pieces. Experts can do this. They can read between the lines to see what brings all of the information together and gives it a coherence. They do not have better memories than novices, or more intelligence, they have simply become familiar with the underlying rules and patterns that predominate in their area of expertise.

To try:

You can test just how much of a presentation people remember. For a talk that you are due to give, make a careful note of all of the points that you intend to make, i.e. all of the examples, facts, figures, graphs, ideas, demonstrations and even anecdotes that will be used. Make a note, also, of who will be in the audience. Do not tell them that you will be testing their memory of the event at a later stage.

At different intervals after the presentation, ask different members of the audience (a few at a time to get an averaging effect) to write down everything they can remember you saying. Give them just a few minutes to do this. Carry this survey out after one day, one week, one month, three months, six months and a year if possible, using different people each time. It is interesting to note just how much people forget, but it is more important to look at what they remember. Do the items remembered correspond to your key points and aims for the presentation? If not, look again at your structure (introduction and conclusion in particular) and see if you can better organise your talk so that the main parts will stick, even after the details have faded away.

It is important that a presentation has the same underlying pattern, and more importantly, that you bring this pattern to the attention of your audience. You are the expert, remember, so it is your job to see the underlying structure and highlight this to the non-experts in the audience.

At a European research project meeting a representative of the EU commission gave a presentation on what is expected of the partners when working on such a project. He presented for an hour and explained many different facets of how the commission runs projects of this kind. At one stage, a comment that he made about the auditing of accounts started to draw questions from the floor. With every answer, there came a further volley of questions and yet further discussion and disquiet. It turned out that a set of independently audited accounts would have to be submitted at the end of the first year of the project and the penalty for default on this submission would be the suspension of all further funding. This was a new development and one that had clearly surprised many, if not most, of the partners.

This was the part of the presentation that was provoking the greatest interest from the audience, so it is reasonable to say that it was the most important item. The rest of the talk covered issues that people either knew already or didn't care to know. The presenter had taken the brief of 'informing people about working on EU projects' far too literally and was giving a summary of this information in several ordered sections. However, what would have been really useful was a talk that highlighted the important issues for the partners to consider in the coming months. Instead of presenting a body of information, the speaker should have highlighted the important or worrisome issues from within that body of information.

All of this information was of course written down somewhere, and all who were at the presentation could have found it if they had searched hard enough. But in this regard, they were effectively 'novices', and this was all just small-print and detail. Yes, the audience *could* have found the necessary information independently, but it would have been very difficult to do so, and they might still have difficulty in working out the implications of it.

The same occurs when consulting a point of law. You can find any law that you want to find – it's all public information – but do you know where to start looking, and can you make sense of the particular law when you manage to track it down? To the presenter, however, the relevant information is a clearly patterned field of knowledge from which

5. Structure

he can easily extract what is important, and only what is important, and present and explain this to the audience.

This role of the presenter as expert is vital. If the presenter does not draw attention to the key conclusions, the audience will form their own. In many cases, if the details form no discernible pattern, then when the details fade from memory nothing will remain at all.

At a presentation course, during a discussion about the use of analogies to help communicate ideas, one person was sceptical, saying that there was no need for tools like this and that 'the facts should speak for themselves'. But think of this in the context of an election. As various counts come in, political commentators are needed to analyse the results for the general public. In a proportional representation system, it can take days for the final results to be announced, and even though detailed, clear, and promptly updated information is available on the Web, it's very difficult for the public to draw accurate conclusions from it without an expert opinion. Raw data is hard to interpret – in short, facts never speak for themselves, or more accurately, you need a presentation for those occasions when the facts *don't* speak for themselves.

Figure 5.6. It's the job of the expert not to present data, but to present conclusions about that data. Political analysts take the vast quantities of data that flood in on election night and inform the viewer what it all means.

Presentations are often given for the wrong reasons, but one occasion when you do require someone to stand up and speak is when there

Key points:

Decide on a conclusion based on your aim for the presentation.

Set a clear context for the presentation – where you wish to take the audience and why – by means of a functional introduction.

A list of topics that you intend to talk through may not, of itself, function as a context-setting introduction.

A story, quotation, demonstration, example, engaging fact or picture are all excellent ways to get interest and set context at the start of a presentation.

Only a few overall ideas – if any – will be remembered from an oral presentation.

is a body of information (be it a lengthy EU report or a mass of election results) that the intended audience cannot easily decipher for themselves. In instances such as these, it is really useful to have an expert on hand to make sense of it all, to guide you to the conclusions that you couldn't draw for yourself, to see the wood from the trees. These insights will be useful, and will be remembered.

6. GUIDE NOTES

After the last chapter you should have a good idea of what is involved in structuring your material. The presentation now has a clean line of attack. You have decided what you want to achieve and how you will attempt to reach this goal. With the plan written out, you must now think about a way to keep yourself to this plan throughout the talk.

The first question to ask is whether you need to have guide notes at all. Is it not more polished to speak without them? The simple answer is no. The greatest political speakers use notes when they speak, so why shouldn't you? It shows respect for your audience that you have prepared a coherent talk and you are making sure to deliver it properly. And to completely lose your way for the want of a set of notes is an unnecessary disaster. But what form should the guide notes take?

Figure 6.1. Even the greatest political speakers use guide notes, and so should you.

This is not such a straight-forward question, and people use very different approaches. On the one hand, there are those that have many dense pages of text in front of them; on the other, there are those who have a few key words jotted on a single page. Both systems come with their perils. The detailed approach can let you down if you get into a flow and then lose your way. When you look down to get a prompt, you are faced with a mass of written information and it is difficult to know where you are. The

Tips on guide notes:

1. Only write on one side of the page.

2. Don't fidget with the notes but place them beside you or in front of you. If you have to hold them, try to make them as solid as possible (use a board or a folder) as flapping wavy notes draw too much attention to themselves, and can end up in tatters at the end of a nervous presentation.

3. Don't read directly from what you have in front of you. People are there to listen to you, the real you. So glance at your guide notes to get your bearings, then look the audience in the eye, and speak to them directly.

sparse approach can cause problems too. You may glance down to gain instruction only to find a single cryptic word like 'next' or 'analyse', which could leave you wondering 'Next what?' or 'Analyse what?'

The problem with these approaches is that they both use a fairly indirect form of visual prompting: written English. This has to be read and decoded before it will jog your memory.

A more direct approach, which will work well for a lot of people, is to use pictures. A picture allows your brain to make a direct visual integration of the prompt. When you see something you know what it is. In Figure 6.2 are several pictures taken from a talk on mechanical vibrations and resonance. Can you guess what each one represents?

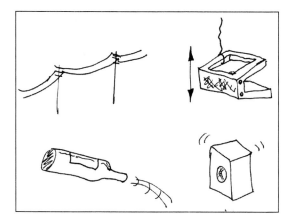

Figure 6.2. Icons or pictures are a good way to cue memory, particularly if you have drawn the pictures yourself.

The easiest one to recognise is the telegraph wires in the top left corner. Below this is beer issuing from a bottle in intermittent glugs, the way it does in television advertisements. The picture on the bottom right is a washing machine, vibrating. Most difficult of all is the picture on the top right, a paper punch on the end of an elastic band, which was a prompt to the speaker to show a vibrating demonstration. And here lies an important point: to very few people is the blob a paper punch, but to the person who sketched it, it is unmistakable. If you draw the pictures yourself, you will remember what you were trying to draw, and it is a very effective form of cueing for this reason. In this case, a quick glance at the guide notes was all the speaker needed to remember to introduce his demonstration.

6. Guide Notes

Even if you really cannot draw you can still use this form of visual prompting. You can use clipart or pictures or photographs. And even words on their own without pictures can be visually enhanced with the addition of colour. Colour divides up a visual field effortlessly. It lifts different areas of text clear of one another. So you might have one colour for visual aids, another for when you want to take a break or ask the audience a question, another for when you want to recap. Some examples is shown in Figure 6.3 below.

Key points:

Always have guide notes with you when you present.

Pictures can cue memory and provide a better prompt than just text alone.

Figure 6.3. You don't have to be able to draw to avail of the powerful visual cueing of images.

With experience, you will worry less and less about guide notes. This does not mean that you will not need to use them, but rather that you should be happy to take a second to consult notes during a presentation. Many presenters are afraid to stop talking for even a few seconds. The sound of silence can induce panic in a nervous presenter, but it shouldn't. Few audiences mind if you take a short break. Remember that listening is always hard work, and it's better to get things right than to keep speaking at all times.

There is another reason why guide notes should become less of a worry, which was explored in the last section of the previous chapter: 'What will be remembered'. The point was made that the details of the talk will be quickly forgotten and only the main ideas will remain. You should see a presentation more as a short list of chunks rather than a long list of individual bullets and, broken up in this way, there will be less bits to have to remind yourself to say.

7. VISUAL AIDS

This chapter focuses on the one thing that really distinguishes a presentation from all other forms of communication – visual aids.

One of the most important points about visual aids has already been stated, and that is that you should only turn your attention to the preparation of visual material *after* you have decided exactly what you are going to say. This sounds logical enough – decide what you wish to say, and then how, and then with what aids – but many presenters do it the other way around. They gather together a set of visuals, and then speak about each one in turn, using the slides to prompt them in each case. It is important that you develop a storyline for your talk in advance of choosing your visual aids.

This chapter highlights five areas to consider when preparing your visual material. At the end of the chapter there are a few comments on PowerPoint which, for better or worse, dominates business presentations in the world today.

Words

It may strike you as ironic that the very first thing discussed in a chapter on graphical material is words. And yet, there is no doubt that the majority of slides used in presentations are made up of words, usually in the form of bullet points. So it would be remiss not to mention this 'graphical tool', as it is so popular among presenters.

Figure 7.1. This famous Bob Dylan video could almost be a parody of the modern-day bullet-point presentation, with every point the speaker makes being paraphrased as he speaks them.

Simply put: a group of words is not a visual aid. The words you produce orally can be inflected, projected, stressed and repeated. They can be complemented with facial expression, body movement and eye contact. They can be brought to life with enthusiasm, passion and belief. And you don't need to take acting lessons to do this. If you speak on a topic in which you are knowledgeable, with a purpose that you have taken the trouble to define, then your conversational instincts will take over and your words will come alive. So why simply reproduce these words drably on each slide? What does this add?

Words written on slides are not just unproductive, they are actually counterproductive. The audience cannot read and listen at the same time, so if you are constantly publishing your points in written form on the screen, you are actively distracting the audience from listening to you.

An important point should be stressed here. This kind of presentation is one where there is a constant stream of bullet-point slides in parallel with the oral delivery. The bullet points come to dominate the presentation in a way that makes the presenter less effective, and this practice is strongly discouraged. It is not the case, however, that you should never use bullet points, or that text should never appear on visual aids – there are times when text can and should appear.

Often it will be necessary to present a list of items, for example as the main areas that you will cover in your talk. This kind of outline slide is very useful for the audience as it provides them with a map of where the presentation will go, and you may even reintroduce this slide at other points in the talk to remind them of this plan. Indeed this kind of re-orientation can be quite important in a presentation because, unlike a report, an audience cannot turn back a few pages to remind themselves of something you said earlier. But these bullet points should be short and concise. You should think of them as a set of headings for what you are going to say. The content of the point in each case is delivered verbally – possibly with the help of other visual material – but the text on the screen is limited to a caption of just a few words, which acts as a label for this point.

Bullet points – like demonstrations, pictures, graphs or diagrams – should be seen as just one of the many tools that you make use of to help you to say what you wish to say. If they help you to communicate they should be used, but to assume that they should be present at all times is wrong. This is deciding on the mode of communication in advance of deciding what you wish to communicate. Certainly they will be useful on some occasions, but surely not all.

Some people offer the argument in favour of bullet points that if you read something, in addition to hearing it verbally, then you will be more likely to remember it. In a general sense, this is valid. It is linked to the idea that the more levels on which you engage with a subject, the more memorable it will be. So if, for example, you went on first aid course, and you just listened to the instructor, this wouldn't be quite as memorable as a course on which you also got to practise resuscitation on a dummy, spoke with an emergency crew, and carried out group brainstorming exercises. The idea goes that the more levels on which you process an idea, the more connections it will form in your brain, and the more rich and memorable will be the overall experience.

This is called *elaborative encoding*, and it is this very process that makes the use of demonstrations so effective, as will be shown in Chapter 16. So, could the same logic not apply to the use of bullet points, where you are listening and reading at the same time? Unfortunately this is not the case. Certainly the use of pictures in tandem with spoken words adds an extra dimension to what you are communicating, but written words on their own do not do this. That is not to say that written media is not powerful, but a set of bullet points that appear as someone is speaking doesn't harness this power.

For example, as you read this piece, it may be provoking you to think about these issues. However, this is not a set of bullet points. It takes quite a few sentences and quite a bit of time to put even the simplest of ideas into print if they are to be in any way engaging or believable. In person the same points could be articulated far more easily and quickly. The real strength of written media is that it is permanent, and you, the reader, can go back to it again and again. It can also be very detailed.

Take, for example, a full-page newspaper spread summarising the results of a British general election. The results of the ballot for all 646 seats are presented on a large coloured map along with the names of each of the constituencies. It is extremely information-rich and a very well-designed visual aid, but totally unsuitable for a presentation. Written media can do lots of things that presentations cannot do so well and vice versa, but bullet points don't harness the strengths of written media (permanent, information-rich) in any substantial way.

Worse, however, than the distraction bullet points can be to the audience, is the far bigger distraction they can be to the presenter. The single biggest factor in the wrong-headedness of most present-day business presentations is the breaking up of the entire talk into a long serious of sections and sub-sections and ultimately bullet points. This can turn a potentially engaging speaker into a robot. Each bullet point acts as a cue for the delivery of a point of information and they follow one another in a long flat procession that overwhelms and under-engages the audience.

An audience will only remember a few key messages from a presentation. The structure of the talk should be built around these key messages so as to bring them cleanly to the audience. Start with this plan and then pick the diagrams, examples, demonstrations, stories, graphs and pictures that will help you to make each point. Many people, however, start with the bullet points. A presentation and a PowerPoint file are seen as one and the same thing, and the creation of the PowerPoint file becomes the primary focus. This is wrong. You should decide on they aim of your talk first, then how you are going to go about achieving this aim, and then, and only then, what visual aids and bullet points may help you to do this.

Another instance where it is beneficial to include words on a visual aid is when you include a quotation. A quote is effectively a highly concise thought-point that makes the audience stop and think. In this case it's the words, often the exact words, that count, and you should give everyone plenty of time to read what you have put up. You should also not talk for the few seconds it takes them to do this, as it is both distracting and irritating.

There is one last point on words that is often brought up and should be addressed. Quite often people take the slides they will use in their presentation, print them out (sometimes two or four to a page) and distribute them to the audience as a useful record of the presentation. If most of the bullet points are stripped from the slides as advocated, then how useful will such a record be? It is amazing how often this point is raised and it is again indicative of how muddled people's thinking about presentations can be. The answer to the problem is simple. Give the audience a handout by all means, but why insist on it being an exact facsimile of the slides?

Suppose you missed a big football match and you wanted to catch up on what had happened afterwards. Let's say that you have two options: either watch the highlights on television that night or read the match report in the newspaper the following morning. Both are different renderings of the same event. On the one hand, on television you

To try:

The next time you are attending a presentation that contains a lot of visual aids and the usual abundance of bullet points, take some time to watch the audience. Observe how much time they spend looking at the presenter and how much time they spend looking at the screen.

can actually see the action with your own eyes, which is fairly compelling but sometimes in a highlights programme you don't get a fair idea of the overall balance of play. On the other hand, the newspaper report might be more descriptive and insightful on this and on other aspects of the game, but you have to rely on your imagination to picture the action for yourself. The point is that each is a very different thing. It would not, for example, be acceptable for the newspaper reporter to simply print a transcript of the commentary from the television programme as his match report. This would not be a very edifying written piece.

Making the slides act as the written report of the presentation will compromise the presentation, or the report, or both. It is like that absurd saying, 'The book is better than the film,' or words to that effect. This is a bit like saying that the smell of a rose is nicer than the colour pink. A book is a book, and a film is a film, and the two are not comparable. Likewise a presentation is a live event and a report is a written document – both can compliment each other in an overall communication task, but the creation of each should be seen as a totally separate task.

Directing Attention

The old adage, 'A picture is worth a thousand words,' is true, but inherent in it is a warning to all presenters, and that is: Do you know which of the thousand words the audience are receiving, and are they the ones you want to communicate? Put another way, when we look at a picture, we all see something different and it is vital that the presenter directs the audience to view what he or she wants them to view.

For example, when you buy a new car you may suddenly notice a proliferation of the same colour and model on the roads. When you wear glasses for the first time, you suddenly start to 'see' all of the other bespectacled people you wouldn't have before. We become filters for our own interests and preoccupations and the same picture can say different things to different people.

It is important, therefore, to direct the audience to what you wish them to see. But there is an easy and a hard way to do this. The hard way is to put up a graph or picture or diagram and then verbally explain what you wish to show, apologising for the lack of clarity, telling the audience to disregard certain details and painstakingly pointing out the key features. The easier way is to render the visual aid in such a way as to make the key point as self-evident as possible. This leaves you with less explaining to do.

It is staggering how often people fail to do this. A visual aid is taken from a particular source, and used in this exact form in a presentation. It is very often the case that the visual aid in its original location is not perfectly formatted for the presentation – why would it be? – and yet it often doesn't occur to the presenter to adapt or reproduce the visual to make it more suitable. This is particularly true of graphs, as will be shown later. For now, the guiding principles for directing attention in visual aids can be stated as follows:

1. Take out anything that doesn't need to be there.
2. Allow the viewer to see what is important as directly as possible.
3. Show one thing at a time.

1. Take out anything that doesn't need to be there – The first principle is obvious. Remove any footnotes, designs or patterns that don't do any work. Edward Tufte, who has written several excellent books on the presentation of graphic material, calls this the principle of 'data-ink'. He says that the proportion of ink on a graphic that is conveying information should be as large as possible. Essentially ink that does no work shouldn't be there. So grids, hatching, boxes, borders, logos and background-slide templates all fall under the axe. Everything on the page should do some work, otherwise it may draw attention to itself for the wrong reason and confuse the audience.

Two graphs are pictured in Figure 7.2. They show the same data but the one on the right has been stripped of a lot of the unnecessary rubbish present in the graph on the left. A slide containing a graph or a picture should only contain that graph or picture.

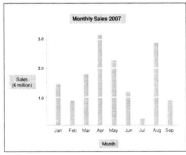

Figure 7.2. Two versions of the same graph, with and without the bells and whistles that so often accompany visual material.

As well as removing distracting material, this will also allow you to render the graphic as large as possible. Figure 7.3 below shows what is all too often seen in presentations, namely the picture playing second fiddle to the slide template. The slide on the left might be considered to be well composed if it were a poster, or found in a magazine, but in a presentation if you wish to show a picture, just show the picture, as demonstrated by the slide on the right. The picture on the left-hand slide occupies less than one sixth of the total area of the page.

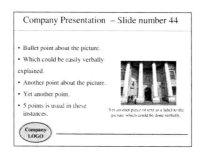 

Figure 7.3. When showing a picture or a graph, allow it to take centre stage and use up as much of the available space as possible, like the slide on the right.

2. Allow the viewer to see what is important as directly as possible – To explain this point, it is first necessary to explain some of the principles of Gestalt psychology. Gestalt psychology became prominent in Germany in the 1920s and 1930s and it studied the way the mind perceives details and brings them together into unified wholes. For example, what do you see in Figure 7.4? No doubt you can instantly perceive two triangles but in neither case is a triangle actually drawn.

Figure 7.4. You can see two triangles in the above figure, even though no triangle is drawn.

Gestalt psychology has outlined several rules for how the mind integrates parts into unified wholes in this way. The above triangles are examples of what is known as *closure*. There are several other principles but, for the purposes of making presentations, only a few are relevant. These are demonstrated in Figure 7.5. The picture on the left is an example of *similarity*. People will always see this pattern as three rows rather than three columns as the objects in the rows are similar. The pattern on the right will usually be interpreted as three pairs of lines rather than six lines, due to the *proximity* of each line pair. Both Gestalt visual integrations are aided by another, which is called *simplest interpretation*.

SIMILARITY   PROXIMITY

Figure 7.5. You will no doubt see the pattern on the left as three rows rather than three columns due to the similarity of the objects along the rows. You will probably see the pattern on the right as three pairs of lines rather than six lines, due to their proximity of the paired lines to each other.

What does this mean for visual aids? This can be shown by the graph in Figure 7.6. It could have been taken straight from Excel and it looks very like many of the graphs that you will have seen in presentations.

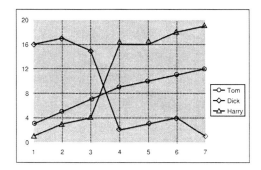

Figure 7.6. A typical Excel graph. By default it has a grey background, gridlines and a legend.

The titles and labels have been removed as they don't concern us here, but obviously such words, unlike many of the bullet points mentioned earlier, would be justified and helpful. The first question to ask is whether all of the gridlines and the coloured background are needed. Are they doing any work or are they just decorations? To answer that question you need to ask another: What is the graph for? In this case, let us say that it is the shape of the graph that is important, not the absolute values of the data, so the gridlines can go, as can the default grey background.

What about the legend? Well, here is where Gestalt psychology comes in. Legends appear on nearly every graph that you see in both presentations and reports, and yet they are actually totally counterproductive. The tenets of Gestalt psychology would say that things that are close together will be grouped and things that are similar will also be grouped. So why not have the labels close to and similar to the things they are labelling, instead of removed off to a legend?

If you look at any map, nearly everything is labelled directly. The name beside the town is the name of the town. Simple. And yet this it not what is happening in the above graph. Also, the town names are all grouped by a common colour. The county names will be a different colour, the rivers another, and the historical sites yet another again. The similarity in colour – and sometimes font size or even font type – groups similar items and distinguishes them from one another. Only the most detailed city streetmaps would resort to a numbered legend, and this for only the smallest lanes and alleyways. In a presentation, however, if you are at this density of information you have already totally over-reached.

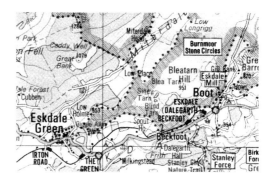

Figure 7.7. Maps use different font sizes and font types to group different items, and everything is labelled directly, but the main tool for associating like features is colour. Without the layering effect that colour provides, the above map looks impossibly cluttered, and yet in its normal form can be read easily.

The same thing happens to an audience at a presentation. Scanning between the legend and the graph becomes tiresome and they lose interest, and the earlier graph is extremely simple by comparison with what is often presented. In any case, presenters rarely allow the audience enough time to digest what they have shown, so even the eager audience member can get left behind. It is better if the visual integration can happen as directly as possible. To this end, the graph from 7.6 has been redrawn in Figure 7.8 to make it easier on the eye and quicker to assimilate.

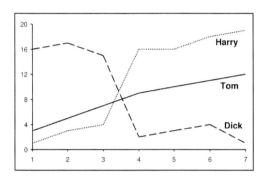

Figure 7.8. The graph from 7.6 is redrawn without the unnecessary and distracting attributes, and with direct labelling. Ideally, it would also use like-coloured fonts to allow direct visual integration.

3. Show one thing at a time – The third principle to mention is a simple, albeit extremely important one. It is easy to overwhelm an audience with a rich visual aid, and it is easy to do this without even knowing that you've done it. The schematic shown in Figure 7.9 demonstrates the point.

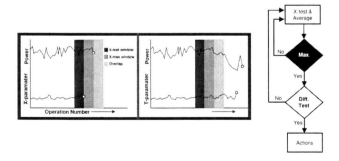

Figure 7.9. This schematic has comparisons going in several directions, which can overwhelm a non-expert audience.

The presenter in this case began by referring to 'the second of the two graphs'. But this is confusing. Is the second graph the one on the far right or the right-hand side of the main graph (in the box on the right), or the graph line on the bottom (within a given particular window)? The speaker continued, and began to discuss the second window. At first you might think that this is the right-most of the boxes, but on closer inspection you realise that within each box there were three 'filter windows' and maybe this is what was meant. As it turned out, the flowchart on the far right showed the audience where they were in the presentation, but this only became obvious several slides into the talk.

Comparisons can be made in several directions on this visual aid and this will confuse the audience. The solution is simple, introduce one idea at a time. PowerPoint comes into its own here, as you can animate the items on a slide and control how and when they appear and disappear. In this way you can introduce features one by one, make other items disappear or fade into the background, move things around the screen from slide to slide, highlight important features, and label things clearly and directly. Be careful not to let these actions distract from your message, but if you think 'explain one thing at a time', then you are far less likely to overwhelm the audience.

Pictures

Until very recently, putting pictures into a presentation was awkward. Digital cameras and scanners were expensive, files were large and difficult to handle, picture quality was poor, and the digital projectors necessary to view these images were few and far between. Things have moved on, however. You can now purchase a digital camera for about the same price as a good dinner for two. You can take excellent-quality pictures and then get a photograph from the camera into a presentation file in a couple of minutes. Pictures from reports, magazines or books can be captured by a scanner, which costs even less than the camera. And then there is the abundance of pictures on the internet. Putting a picture into a presentation has never been easier.

Pictures work in several ways. Many of these should be obvious to the reader but one or two in the following list may not have occurred to you.

- Make ideas tangible – A picture will make an abstract idea real. An audience will always welcome seeing a picture of what you are talking about.

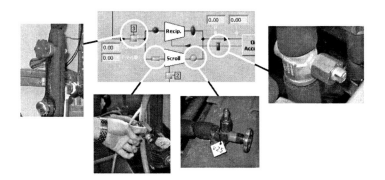

Figure 7.10. The above figure was taken from a presentation where the aim was to explain the schematic in the centre. In order to make the icons more real to the audience, small photographs were used as shown. This was also paralleled with physical demonstrations of each of the items pictured. Needless to say, the above diagram was built up step by step.

- Break for the audience – Even if a picture doesn't do a lot of work in the presentation, it does no harm either. Sometimes presenters use pictures at the start of each section of their talk: each picture is no more than a title slide but it acts like a punctuation mark, telling the audience that a new section is beginning. Little breaks like this are not just good for alerting the audience of the sections in your talk, but they also give everyone a small breather.
- Getting attention – This was covered in the section 'Selling the Presentation' in Chapter 5. Pictures are very evocative. You only have to flick through any newspaper to see photographs being used in this way.
- Memory – If a picture grabs your attention, then it is more likely to stay in your memory. Visual memory is very powerful compared to other senses. A picture will often be one of the few that the audience remembers from your talk.
- Another level – The more levels on which you process an idea, the more memorable and engaging it will be. So, as well as explaining an idea verbally, if you also see a picture, answer a question and carry out a role-playing exercise, then the idea will form a more elaborate set of connections in your brain and be more memorable. The easiest additional level to include on top of the purely verbal is the visual.
- Easy for you – It can take hours to put together an elaborate

To try:

Watch the news on television with the sound turned down. Notice how many visual images there are that aren't strictly necessary. If there is a feature about air travel, there will be images of aeroplanes landing and taking off, people checking in, and shots of the terminal building. If there is a report on schools, there will be pictures of children playing in a playground, a teacher talking in a classroom, a child bent over a copy book writing, and so on. None of these visuals are strictly necessary; viewers could just as easily understand the content of the story without them. However, people like to look at pictures, even if they only act as a breather.

diagram when the same visual argument can made more clearly by including a picture. This is not always the case, but even in situations where a diagram (maybe showing a cut-away to see the inner workings of a machine) is more suitable, why not include a picture as well? In a written document, this may increase your printing workload, but in a presentation, throwing in four or five extra photographs is no trouble at all.

Graphs

When asked what they would like to improve on, presenters most often mention such things as tackling nerves, how to structure the material, how to keep the attention of the audience, and how to keep on track and stay focused. No one ever says: 'I need help with my graphs, they're ineffective and confusing to the audience.' And yet the misuse of graphs is one of the most common faults of presentations.

The reason that presenters don't notice that they have a problem with their visual aids is the reason that this problem exists in the first place. People look on their own graphs the way proud parents look at their child. There is a filtering process that takes place, which only allows them to see what they want to see.

A similar process is demonstrated in Figure 7.11. At first glance it just looks like a mess of black and white blobs. However, on closer inspection, a Dalmatian dog can be seen. Once the dog has been 'spotted' it is very difficult to imagine not being able to see it, or more to the point, it becomes very easy to ignore all of the distracting blobs in the background.

Figure 7.11. Can you make out the animal in this picture? Once you know what to look for, it is easy to pull the foreground object from the background details

When a presenter puts a graph into a presentation, he or she often doesn't realise how much information is being presented, and how much of it the expert presenter finds it easy to ignore. It can be very difficult for the audience to see exactly what they are supposed to see, like the dog in the above figure.

To demonstrate this, consider the simple plot shown in Figure 7.12. The question is, what attributes of the graph can alter your conclusion about what you are seeing? Or, put another way, what features of the graph in Figure 7.12, if changed, could totally change the overall meaning of the graph?

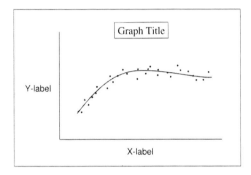

Figure 7.12. In this fairly simple single-variable plot, how many features of the above figure could significantly alter the message that the graph conveys?

Well, you can probably come up with a few answers to this question straight away. Firstly there is the graph title, as well as the titles on both the X and Y axes. To compliment the written titles, there would be a verbal description of the graph, when the presenter tells the audience what the graph is about. These things are obvious and if everything was well labelled and well described, these should be clear to the audience.

So let's move on to the small-print. What do you see when you look at the two graphs pictured in Figure 7.13? The first is similar to the graph in 7.12. What about the one on the right? Without having a context by which to judge this data, it is of course impossible to know, but it may surprise you to learn that the graph on the right is plotted from exactly the same data as that on the left. The only difference is the scale and zero position on the Y-axis. This totally changes the shape, and therefore the immediate visual impression that the graph makes.

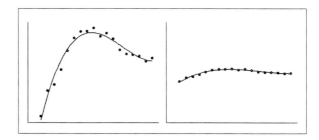

Figure 7.13. These two graphs make very different visual impressions, but they are in fact plotted from the same data set. The difference is due to the choice of scaling and zero point on the Y-axis.

This may seem like an obvious visual deception, but it is one that is often missed by presenters. In fact, like many of the oversights examined here regarding graphs, presenters usually aren't even aware that they have led the audience astray. None of this is helped by the fact that Excel, by default, will autoscale your X and Y axes for you. If you are showing multiple plots for comparison purposes, how much of the contrast is due to data, and how much is due to the way the data is rendered? The audience will only get the chance to make a quick visual inspection and this vitally important factor might be lost on them.

This brings us to another important attribute of the graph, probably the most important of all: the shape. The real strength of any graph is the ability to take hundreds, even thousands, of data points and render them in one simple form. We can make an appraisal of this form using our skills of visual integration, coupled with some background knowledge. The shape of the graph is like an identifying signature.

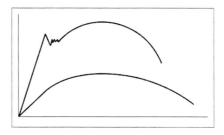

Figure 7.14. Shape is one of the key attributes of any graph. The real power of a graph is to take a large volume of numbers and transform them into a visually examinable form. A materials engineer, for instance, would be able to tell a lot about the curves above just by making a quick inspection of their shape.

Pictured in Figure 7.14 are the load-extension curves from tensile tests carried out on two different metals. The point here is that if you were familiar with this field, you would be able to tell, just by glancing at the shape of each graph that the upper curve is from a carbon steel, whereas the lower is from a more ductile metal, possibly brass. Also, from the shape of the graph alone, comparative estimates of the metal's stiffness, toughness and ductility could be made.

Shape is probably the most striking feature of any graph. Heart specialists can look at a complex ECG trace and diagnose many different heart defects. Meteorologists can look at weather maps and tell you where the rain will fall. These diagnoses are made based on shape and form. Obviously, your audience must be able to interpret these forms themselves if they are to be useful levers for your argument, but the point is that the shape of the graph is a potentially important attribute, so this is one of many things that can draw the audience's attention. Is this what you want?

Sometimes only certain portions of a graph are significant. For example, in 7.14, one of the most important areas of the graph is the region on the far left (a straight-line section for all metals). In this region, the material is elastic. It acts like a spring. The stiffness of this spring can be estimated from the steepness or slope of this portion of the graph. Is this the feature you wish to concentrate on? Do the audience know that you wish them to focus their attention here?

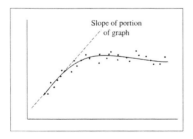

Figure 7.15. The slope, or steepness, of some portion of a graph can be an important attribute.

Going back to our original graph in 7.15, is the slope of the initial (or indeed any) portion of the graph of interest? There are other features of slope such as points of inflection and even saddle points, not to mention second and third derivatives of the slope. And related to slope is the maximum or peak value of the graph. So, for example, if this were a graph of noise levels on a busy street, the peak recorded value might become the important feature. Then there are the start and end points of the graph, which themselves may indicate something important. As you can see, this simple graph could have quite a few key features, depending on the data it represents.

Suppose the above was a graph of yearly rainfall, over the second half of a calendar year, and let's say that each data point is the weekly rainfall value averaged over 30 years of records. So what would be important in this instance? Well, again it depends on your audience and your aim. If you were interested in climate change, you might compare the average value of the entire chart over the whole year and compare it to the average value 30 years ago. If you were a farmer, you would again be interested in the average rainfall, but maybe only in particular seasons, as shown on the right-hand graph of Figure 7.16.

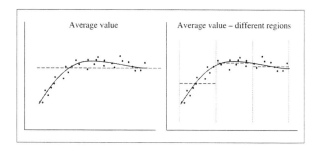

Figure 7.16. The overall level of the graph or portions of the graph can be an important feature.

Suppose you were to find out that the average daily rainfall in August was 2 mm per day and you were planning a wedding for this time of year. Would it be reasonable to assume that there will be 2 mm of light drizzle in the morning and the rest of the day will be fine? The weather is a classic example of where there is an average value and random variation or scatter about this average. On a given (unlucky) day in August, there could be a couple of inches of rain and a very soggy wedding reception. Very often scatter is a more important feature than overall trend, as it shows the precision of the data that was used to draw up this trend.

You will notice in the original graph that there is a considerable scatter of points, but a best-fit line is drawn through them. How was this decided? The graph could have been plotted by simply joining the dots, instead of fitting the curve that is shown. Alternately, a different type of curve could have been fitted, such as one of a different order allowing for more kinks. Several of these possibilities are shown in Figure 7.17. The choice originally made, of using a third-order polynomial (a curve with two turning points) is probably the best one for capturing the general trend of this data set, but does the audience know this? Is it an important assumption? Is it a reasonable assumption? If so, shouldn't you mention it? If not, will it distract and confuse the audience unnecessarily? Does your audience even understand the whole concept of first and second order curve-fits? The number of questions that this simple graph provokes is growing.

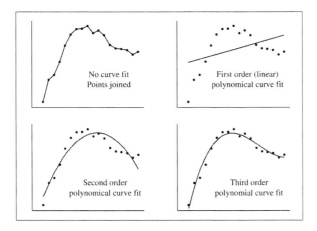

Figure 7.17. The way you interpolate between data points is yet another important attribute of a graph.

You can ask yet more questions. What was the source of the data? What calculations were carried out? What was the sample size? Was the data normalised? How do these results compare with previous data? How do they compare with the baseline? And remember, this is a single-plot graph – just one variable plotted along two dimensions. If you introduce even one extra plot then your audience may be left wondering about the comparisons between the two graphs – level, shape, slope – or the significance of any point of intersection, or the colour of the plot-lines or the different tick marks used, and so on.

It's usually true that this multitude of features is not always confusing to the audience. For example, if a group of metallurgists were told they were going to be shown the results from a tensile test, and were then shown Figure 7.14, they would know exactly what to look out for and what to ignore. But very often the audience will not bring this background knowledge to bear on what they are seeing, and you should be aware that even a simple graph contains a great many potentially key features, and most graphs that appear in presentations are, alas, a great deal more complex and less clearly rendered than those shown here. The lesson is simple: as the expert, it is the presenter's job to lead the audience patiently and clearly to the important features of any graph that he or she uses.

Graphs are the communication tool that presenters most often abuse. But used carefully, these deceptively simple visual aids can be powerful tools for conveying large volumes of numeric data.

Slide Sentences

Visual aids are supposed to help you to communicate your message to the audience but, if poorly chosen, they can in fact have the opposite effect: distracting the audience and even the presenter. The way to avoid this is to write down a single sentence that states what each visual aid is trying to achieve. This is called a *slide sentence.*

Doing this will really clear your head on the whole issue of visual aids and will bring a clarity (and often simplicity) to your slides that most people needlessly fail to achieve. Suppose you wish to give a presentation on the workings of a sub-system within a large process in a factory. This process is represented by means of a visual schematic that is familiar to all in the factory. This schematic – shown in Figure 7.18 – you might think would be a good visual image to use in the presentation.

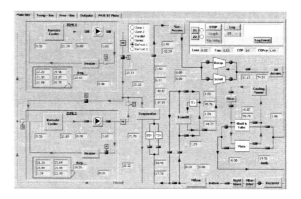

Figure 7.18. This schematic of a process may be used to discuss a sub-system within that process, but is it the most suitable visual aid?

This happens often. In a presentation on a project, the flowchart for the whole project will be shown. In a presentation on a particular building, an architect's plans of that building will be shown. In a presentation on financial estimates, the spreadsheet used to generate these estimates will be shown. This would seem to make sense: you are talking about something so you have that something on view while you speak.

But is this good enough? Is the above schematic a good visual aid? Well, that of course depends on what you wish to communicate. As a title slide it is fine, but if you wish to explain the working of a particular sub-system within the plant, it is not the best choice.

The main problem is that it is far too detailed. It may be the view of the process that people are used to seeing, but is all of the detail necessary for this presentation? A more sensible slide would concentrate on a small portion of the schematic, as shown in Figure 7.19.

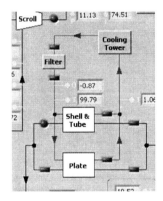

Figure 7.19. A more focused section of the schematic.

This is a little easier to use and a little clearer. However, it may still not be good enough. By zooming in, you have made the items under scrutiny larger, but in some visuals, this may reduce their quality, making them grainy or blurred. Also, you have not eliminated the items that you don't wish to present, and these may distract the audience in the same way discussed in the previous section on graphs. Finally, the original colouring and visual rendering may not be suitable for your purpose here. In short, the original schematic was formatted for one purpose, whereas you are now using it to do a different job. A more suitable visual might be that shown in Figure 7.20, which you can see is very different from the first one used.

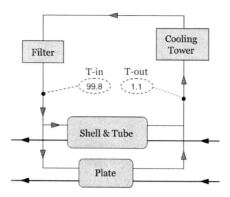

Figure 7.20. Full control has now been taken of the schematic for the purposes of presentation.

By redrawing the diagram on your own terms, you can now show exactly what you want to show, and show it clearly. It is simply a matter of taking control of the visual material so that it communicates what you want it to. Presenters very often don't do this: a graph might be taken from Excel with faint, differently coloured plot-lines, auto-scaled axes, a grey background, thick domineering gridlines and a legend. It's far from ideal, and yet this is the graph that appears in the presentation, copied and pasted, and in no way suitable for the purpose.

The use of visual aids in this way, from their original source and without alteration, can be called *completeness*. It indicates a mindset that says: 'I need to talk about a certain issue, and I have these pictures/graphs/flowcharts/diagrams, so I will present these and explain them as well as I can.' It is a sign of bad planning and is easily remedied by the exercise of writing slide sentences for every one of your visual aids.

There is another error often made by presenters, which is called *correctness*. The problem here is slightly different from that of completeness, and can be paraphrased as: 'I have used a particular proposition to make a point, but let me make a few qualifying remarks on that proposition, just so that I can set all of the records straight.' Academics, lawyers, engineers and generally people who have an eye for detail tend to get snared by this. They say something, and then add several qualifying remarks or facts and figures so they can be correct on all counts. They don't wish to be misinterpreted in any way, but the effect is to distract the audience from the central point of the communication, and overload them with unnecessary information.

Although a predominantly verbal failing, *completeness* also finds its way into visual aids. The problem can occur in several different forms, such as:

- Footnotes and call-outs being used to explain features of slides and diagrams where, if more visually intuitive, the slides could do without these notes.
- Maps and schematics drawn unnecessarily to scale.
- Features that convey useful information in certain situations (e.g. North-south compass indicator, author of drawing) being included in situations where this information is not required.
- Adhering to scientific standards and units in preference to those more familiar to the audience (e.g. quoting pressures in kilopascals instead of in bar, or quoting weight in kilograms instead of in stones).

There are many more, but it may help to explain what is meant by *correctness* and to show just how hard it can be to break away from it. The story of the development of the London Underground map is an interesting one from the point of view of *correctness*. The first underground railway was built in London in 1863. By the 1930s, the system had developed considerably and the map had become extremely complex and thus difficult to use. In 1933, a radical new map was designed by a part-time electrical draughtsman by the name of Harry Beck.

Beck's map differed from previous maps in three important ways. First, all of the lines were drawn as straight lines (vertical, horizontal, or at a 45° angle). This was inspired by Beck's experience of drawing circuit diagrams, where wires are drawn in a functional schematic layout rather than as they appear physically. Second, he removed all of the above-ground detail. The only remaining geographical feature, which acts as a datum for the whole map, is the river Thames, which is itself drawn in schematic form. Third, the scale on the central portion (where there is the greatest concentration of detail) is exaggerated and the scale on the outer portions of the graph is compressed.

The Underground map is a tool. It enables people to get from one part of London to another. The details that were stretched, straightened or eliminated altogether don't contribute to this function, so Beck reasoned that they needn't be shown at all. Yes, most maps have lots of detail and are drawn perfectly to scale, but underground, this information is of little value. It is correctness for the sake of correctness and it only makes things more confusing. Beck realised this because, as a user of the Tube himself, he saw clearly what the goal of the map should be and wasn't afraid to redraw it with this goal clearly in mind.

Beck's map has changed slightly over the years, but the essential design concept has survived and has indeed been copied by several other underground rail systems worldwide. Looking at it now, it is hard to believe that no one came up with the idea earlier, but such can be the mindset of correctness. A map represents geographical reality, so to start bending and stretching features takes you away from standard practice very quickly. And yet this is what you have to sometimes do with visual aids. If you answer 'What is this slide supposed to achieve?' in each case by writing a slide sentence, then it will help you to do this.

As a last point, it should be stressed that although some presenters become consumed by details and lose sight of the overall message, a presentation can never be woolly or inaccurate. Nothing will sink you more quickly than saying something that is plainly erroneous. The details are important, but they serve to bear out your overall arguments, and your overall conclusions. In time, the details will be forgotten, but if you have done your job well, then the key messages will remain. Decide what point you wish to impart with each particular slide and then render that slide so that it carries out this task, and this task alone.

Some Comments on PowerPoint

It would be impossible to complete a chapter on visual aids without mentioning PowerPoint. Indeed it has been mentioned several times already, but it may nonetheless be useful to summarise the various arguments in a balanced way.

The downside – Let's look at the negatives first. These have been mentioned several times already but the argument can be summarised simply by saying that overuse of PowerPoint to show slide after slide of bullet points fails in two ways: it distracts both the audience and the speaker.

It is difficult for an audience to read and listen at the same time. And if there is an engaging speaker – an expert – talking with interest about something that is of use to them, why would they want to read at all? Written material has its strengths and its uses (it is permanent and can be very detailed) but these are not harnessed by fleeting bullet points. The audience gets little out of this and it breaks the essential contact between speaker and listener. Bullet-point slides can be useful, but the quantity of text should be sparse, and they should only be used when really necessary, not continuously throughout the presentation.

Worse, however, is the distraction that PowerPoint is to the speaker. And this is not just the frequent glances at the screen or the necessity to keep clicking the show forward. More damaging is the way it flattens the structure of the presentation. Rather than being an engaging story with three or four key ideas, each one fleshed out with examples, graphs, stories, demonstrations or analogies; it becomes, instead, a long procession of propositions, one after another, and the presenter's delivery can become tedious.

Apart from anything else, there is no justification for this kind of delivery. A presentation is a verbal communication between an individual and a group. The set of speaking skills you have been perfecting for years can thus be employed to great effect with a bit of practise. Why should this always be accompanied by many of the same words, printed out on the screen? Showing pictures, diagrams and occasionally lists and headings is beneficial, but why would you choose to paraphrase everything you say in bullet-point form?

This kind of presentation is often indicative of back-to-front planning. By using PowerPoint slides throughout, you are deciding that this mode of communication is the best mode for communicating everything that you wish to communicate. Instead you should move forward as follows:

- Decide what you want the audience to achieve.
- Decide what ideas or arguments you wish to put forward to realise this.
- Decide (imaginatively) how you will make each point.

If you plan it this way, you will find there is not nearly as big a role for bullet points.

The benefits – Occasionally, you do come across people who say they have no time for PowerPoint and who suggest not using it at all. This is an over-reaction. PowerPoint is not the problem, it is the wrong-headed use of PowerPoint that is the problem. If you think back twenty years, the only way to show pictures in a presentation was to take photographs, develop them, crop them and then send them to a printer to make into slides. These would then be loaded into a slide projector and the presenter would click the slide carousel forward, explaining each one in

To try:

If you have a colleague who is very familiar with the material that you are presenting, try the following. Write down slide sentences for each of the visual aids that you are using. Give these sentences to your colleague and ask him or her to suggest a visual aid that would best serve the purpose embodied in each sentence. Then compare the slides that your colleague envisions with those you have created.

Key points:

For each visual aid, write down in one clear sentence what you wish to achieve.

Remove anything that doesn't contribute to this goal.

Add items to direct the focus of the audience towards this aim.

Use text very sparingly on visual aids.

Take particular care with graphs that the feature you wish to communicate is highlighted.

turn. Text was a problem; labels and arrows were a problem; diagrams were a problem. And then there were all of the perils of jammed projectors, as well as upside-down and back-to-front images, not to mention the almost complete lack of flexibility – a change in order of the slides being about the best you could manage.

Now you can scan the pictures into your computer or load them directly from a digital camera. You can use the computer to alter, add items to, or animate these images. You can also use graphic tools to create images and diagrams of your own. These can all be put together and sequenced in a presentation and, with the aid of a data projector, projected onto a screen for all to see.

You can tailor material for a particular presentation in a very short time. You can build images up in steps and make items appear and disappear, so as to achieve good directed focusing for the audience. The presentation material is then portable and easily assimilated into more detailed written documents. PowerPoint makes the rendering of visual material so easy that it would be foolish not to avail of it when making a presentation.

In summary, PowerPoint, like so many things thrown up by the digital revolution, is a useful tool. However, you must always ask the question, 'What am I trying to achieve?' Then, and only then, turn to PowerPoint to help you to do this, and only when you actually need to.

PART THREE: DELIVERY

The question is often posed: which is more important, preparation or delivery? Some say that preparation is everything and there is no way to cut corners or fool an audience about this, no matter how charismatic and confident a speaker you are. Others point out that all the good material in the world will sink without trace if you cannot sell it to the audience. Both are, of course, correct. The style of the presenter and the quality of what he or she is presenting are like horse and rider in a race: if either is poor, the presentation will be poor. However, although both are equally important, it turns out that you have very little that's *new* to learn about style.

This surprises some people. They feel that they know their subject, and can put slides together and prepare their material, only to find that it all unravels when they go up to speak. They yearn to be able to think and talk clearly, feel and look confident, and to be able to keep the audience's attention; in short, they want to improve their delivery. This may seem like no small task but the important point is, that you already have the necessary skills to make fascinating presentations. They can all be drawn from the vast palette of communication skills that you have been developing almost since the day you were born.

The trick is to tap into this skill-set and to present with the energy and fluency that you would use when telling a friend about your holidays. The way to do this is with practise, and clear-headed and thorough preparation. You will then be able to bring your communication skills from the conversational (one-to-one) to the presentation (one-to-many) domain.

8. EYE CONTACT

This is an extremely important aspect of the communication process. If you don't look at the people in your audience – all of them – they won't feel involved in the presentation. They will feel that you are talking at them, rather than to them, and this will hugely diminish your effectiveness.

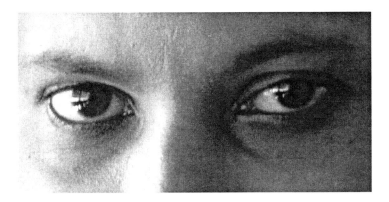

Figure 8.1. Eye contact is a most powerful element of presentation style.

Where Presenters Like to Look

There are several distractions that pull presenters away from their audience and chief among them is the screen. Due to the modern-day obsession with slide-heavy, PowerPoint presentations, attention invariably becomes focused on the screen. Very often it is many times larger than the presenter and such a dominant visual spectacle usually becomes the centrepiece of the presentation. Presenters often compound this problem by looking at the screen themselves, commenting on the visual proceedings like a guide in an art gallery.

The main exhibit in any presentation is you. You are the expert, with useful insights that the audience has turned up to learn. There is nothing more compelling than listening to someone who really knows their topic well. Why deny this to the audience? The visual aids that you use are just that – 'aids' – they aid you in giving the talk but they are not the most important element. Refer to them as they become necessary during the logical progression of your presentation, and then remove them when you have finished with them. Putting yourself first, and the slides second, will encourage you to keep looking at your audience and not at the screen behind you.

Pay attention to group conversations that you are involved in. Does the person who is talking at a given time look at everyone or just at the person they are responding to? Think about yourself as you speak in these situations. Are you glancing around at everyone in the group as you speak?

Good communicators do this automatically. They look at everyone and therefore they make everyone feel involved in the conversation. They may focus a bit more attention on the person they are responding directly to, but they realise that the silent onlookers in the group are also interested in the communication, and are therefore also worthy of their attention. Use the next group conversation you are involved in to make a study of this.

Another place presenters like to look is down. Down at the ground, down at their guide-notes, or down at the screen of their laptop. This is, of course, due to nerves, but again it is very destructive to the communication that you wish to build with the audience. Remind yourself to look up constantly during the presentation and it soon becomes habitual. You will also notice as you do this that seeing the people you are speaking to will force you to slow down and to experience the presentation as more of a conversation and less of a speech.

Some people do make eye contact, but only with a 'chosen few' in the audience. These might be the people who are nodding or who look interested, or it might be the most senior person in the group, or simply the person most obviously in the presenter's line of sight. Although this is better than looking at the screen, or at your feet, it is still not ideal. Those who are not included in your glances around the room will soon start to feel at a distance from the event.

At a recent presentation skills course in a pharmaceutical company, the head of the section was already speaking when one of the participants came into the room. So as not to disturb the presentation, she sat down just inside the door, almost behind the speaker. The speaker continued after a brief pause. Her style was energetic and intense and she looked around at each and every person in the room, almost imploring them to understand and agree with what she was saying. Most tellingly, she even included the latecomer in her field of focus, literally looking over her shoulder to make eye contact. The effect was palpable. Everyone felt intimately involved with the presentation. Everyone felt that the talk was being directed at them, so they were encouraged to sit up and take notice of what was being said.

It is important that you try to involve everyone in the presentation, not just those who seem to be giving you the most encouragement. Respect everyone by looking at everyone; it's that simple.

Do You Look All the Time?

One study on eye contact showed that the speaker makes eye contact 40% of the time, whereas the listener makes eye contact 70% of the time. Whether these figures are exact or not, they do raise an interesting question. If all of the skills of presentation are found in conversation, then how do you account for all of the conversational experiences that don't involve eye contact? After all, the most intimate of friends, in the deepest of conversations, might often look into space or down at their hands when thinking about what they are saying. Can there not be an equivalent of this in a presentation?

The answer is: yes there can, but with two provisos. Firstly, the intimate conversation mentioned above is unrehearsed. It is spontaneous. The two friends may have decided to meet, and they may even have decided in advance what they wanted to talk about, but the exact direction that the communication would take after that was unknown. In a presentation this is not the case. You will have thought out what you are going to say beforehand and, although this should never be learnt off like a speech, it will still move along in a focused way. The time you take to put your ideas into words will give the talk a naturalness and a conversational feel, but you will not be thinking the basic ideas through on the spot. The long pauses that can crop up in a conversation may take place when you are preparing a presentation, but not when you are delivering it.

The second proviso is that although it may be OK for you to break eye contact with the audience from time to time (indeed deliberately taking breaks is a good thing), there are times when full contact is crucial. The simple rule is that you should really lock on to your audience at the start and end of each thought-point.

In other words, when you are introducing a new idea, it is vital that you make a quick scan of the room to alert the audience to the importance of this new idea, and to show them that you believe in what you are going to say. Then, after taking some time to explain this, you might have a concluding statement that rounds that segment off. Again, you must fix contact with the audience at this point to really drive the point home. You may even stop speaking for a few seconds as you look around the room, to allow the point to sink in. If you don't make eye contact at these key moments, you will appear vague and uncommitted. You may also fail to properly alert your audience to the natural division of ideas within your presentation.

Once again, the template for this can be found in any conversation. Suppose you were talking to a friend and he or she asked you a weighty question, such as, 'So, are you going to stay in your job or not?' You would probably look at your friend as they asked the question, carefully taking in what they were saying. Then you would keep your eyes on them as you began your response: 'Well, I think I'll probably stay on.' Then you would expand on your reasons for making this decision; at times looking into space, at times looking at the ground, often looking back at your

Key points:

Make eye contact with everyone in the room.

It is particularly important to focus eye contact on the audience at the beginning and end of your individual thought-points.

friend to read their reaction to what you were saying. Then, as you were wrapping up, you would probably once again look your friend in the eye as you deliver your concluding remarks, saying: 'So, yes, I think it might be best to stay there for now.' Although you would have maintained eye contact for much of the time that you spoke, you would almost certainly have done this at the introduction and at the conclusion of whatever thought-point that you were delivering.

9. CONVERSING WITH THE AUDIENCE

This chapter looks at how you talk to the audience. Imagine the following scenario. Four people are sitting around a table in a restaurant enjoying a meal. They are engaged in an intimate and stimulating conversation. At one point, a member from the group, responding to a remark made from the person across the table, tells a story from her own experience that she feels adds an interesting insight to what they are discussing. She begins by explaining the context of the story in question, what happened, who was involved, how it all began. Over the next three or four minutes, she relates the events of the story, looking around at everyone in the group, pausing, raising and lowering her voice, gesticulating with her hands, reacting to the events she is describing, and finally reaching a conclusion. At this point, she emphasises the important crux (the 'moral' if you like) of the events she has described, and links it to the discussion that prompted the story in the first place. This is a presentation.

You give presentations all the time. If you can sit down among a group of friends and tell them a story over dinner, then what extra abilities do you need to stand in front of a group to make a presentation? People say that it is easy to talk with friends because you don't feel nervous. This is true but, if you give enough presentations, these nerves will subside and you will get used to the sound of your own voice and the feel of speaking to a group, so that it is no longer something that intimidates you. Think about the first time you met those friends, or the time you joined a sports club, or the day you started your current job. You were nervous and intimidated then, but you got used to the people in the group and now you can talk to them effortlessly.

People often also point out that in a conversation, the topics are unplanned and you don't have to remember a long series of things to talk about. Certainly in a longer presentation you might worry about losing your way, so you will have to write out a plan for yourself and use some kind of guide notes, but with a bit of preparation this is easily done. The point is that even a longer presentation is just a set of small 'chunks', each one like the story told over dinner, and you can deliver each of these chunks very easily. Indeed, breaking a presentation into a small set of chunks (where each is a story or an analogy or an example) instead of a long series of bullet points makes for a far more interesting and memorable talk. If you can talk, you can present.

Figure 9.1. There is little difference in the skills used when talking to a group of friends socially and talking to a group in a presentation.

The ability to converse is something that we've been learning almost since we were born. Although most people don't start to speak until they are just over a year old, the action-and-reaction of the communication process starts very soon after birth. And it is not something that we master in a few years; we continue to acquire these skills throughout our lives.

As well as these learnt skills there are the innate skills, such as the massive range of facial expressions and the full lexicon of body language, which adds further colour to the communication process. We possess a truly awesome array of conversational skills for engaging with other human beings. There is precious little else that we have to add to this in order to make a presentation. The trick is to bring your conversational persona into your presentations and to allow the skills that you already possess to shine through. And in order to do this, you must identify and promote your own presentation style.

Styles of Presentation

Everybody is different. Every person talks differently, and thus every person will present differently. Some people are energetic and bubbly; some are ponderous and considered; some are friendly and vivacious; some are serious; some love to answer questions; some people walk about the room; some are the very pattern of composure; some look searchingly into the eyes of everyone in the audience; some fiddle with everything around them and drop the chalk regularly; some smile a lot, some never do; some shout without realising it; some speak low and the audience listens carefully to everything they say.

Whatever your style is, that's your style. If you try to be someone else, it will look utterly false. Your emotions, actions and expressions will not fill out the persona you have invented half as well as they will fill out the real you, and the presentation will be severely compromised.

Figure 9.2. Everyone has a different style, and no one style is better than another. The best style that you can adopt is the one that comes naturally to you.

It is useful to find out a little bit more about your style by asking a trusted colleague or friend to describe how you come across when you are presenting. It is also very useful to see yourself present on video at least once. People often adopt a formal demeanour when presenting. They deliberately turn off parts of their personality in the belief that they are not relevant to the act of presenting. This was earlier referred to as the 'glass box' of presentations, where the presenter is somehow removed from the people in the audience. This will always undermine your talk. Recognise your own unique and very sophisticated conversational style and use it to the full.

Tweaking Your Style

Some readers will wonder if it is really that simple. How can speaking in front of a group of three hundred people be the same as speaking to three friends over dinner? But if you have experience of speaking before a large assembly, after a while it can feel just like talking to a small group of colleagues over a desk. You simply cannot change your style and you cannot afford to discard all of the conversational skills you have spent so long developing. There may, however, be a few small adjustments that you can make to your style in order to facilitate the presentation forum, but these are only adjustments, a slight exaggeration of what is already naturally there. It will be helpful to look at these adjustments under three headings: pace, pitch and volume.

Pace – People often worry that they speak too fast. This problem is compounded by the fact that when they get nervous, most people do speak faster. So, many presentation books ask you to slow down. This is all very well, but have you ever tried to speak slowly? Can you imagine that a deliberate attempt to slow the rate at which words are coming from your mouth is going to sound anything but absurd? And what about style? If it is your natural inclination to speak fast, this can give your delivery great energy and fluency. Where does all of that go if you try to speak in slow motion?

The truth about the rate at which you speak is that an anyone in your audience will be able to hear more quickly than you can speak. It would be nearly impossible for someone to speak a sentence so fast that a normal person, fluent in the same language, could not understand it. The problem is not the rate at which the words are delivered but rather the rate at which the ideas are delivered. If the same quick-fire approach were adopted for the next sentence, and then the next and the next, item after item, a problem would very quickly develop.

When we hear a sentence spoken quickly, we spend a split-second afterwards digesting the meaning of that sentence. If the meaning of the sentence is still not clear, we can actually aurally replay the sentence in our heads by means of what psychologists call the *phonological loop*. This is a mental tape-recording of what we have just heard. You would use it if, say, you wanted to remember a phone number. You would keep saying the number to yourself so that you could hear it in your mind, which keeps the number in the phonological loop until you get around to using it. But if the next idea arrives on top of this, and then the next one again straight after, the brain of the listener quickly chokes up with unprocessed information and listening becomes exhausting. Speaking quickly is not a problem, but you must have pauses in between thought-points to allow the audience to digest the meaning of each.

How do you integrate these pauses into your presentations? There are many ways. One way is to take a sip of water. This looks totally natural and it is very important to keep your vocal chords lubricated if you are speaking for a long time. Another method is to ask a question. Even if you do not wish to get a response, you can ask a rhetorical question.

For example, you may simply say: 'So now that we have explored the problem, how, you may wonder, are we going to go about solving it?' Not only will this allow you to inject a brief natural pause, but the question will act as point of inflection, alerting the audience that you are about to launch into the next stage of the talk.

Another way to have natural-sounding pauses is to move around the room. Presenters are often advised not to move around too much, but unless you are jumping like a loon, a bit of movement adds to a presentation and certainly does it no harm. So you may be talking and then introduce a visual aid, at which point you walk from where you are speaking to the screen to comment on the slide, and then you walk back to where you were originally standing before continuing to speak.

Referring to your guide notes is another way to break up your delivery. Again, some people would suggest that this is bad practice, but it is not. Having a guide for your presentation is essential, even if it only acts as a safety net. If you check on this guide from time to time, it shows that you have prepared carefully and that you have a clear plan. This shows respect for your audience. In all but a very few situations, this will be acceptable. Even during debates in the houses of parliament, the party leaders will bring a large folder of notes to the despatch box each time they speak.

As you grow in confidence, you can put the pauses in at will. It takes a small bit of courage because a short silence can seem like a gaping chasm of uncertainty to a nervous speaker. However it can produce a very powerful effect, particularly when coupled with good eye contact. Suppose you had just made an important point. To really emphasise this statement, you could pause and look around at the people in the room. The pause alerts the audience that you've reached a critical juncture, which will prompt them to review the last thing you have said. Also, the eye contact tells them that you believe in what you are saying and that you are inviting them to consider the idea for themselves. It is as if you are asking, 'What do you think?' With a bit of practise, this technique becomes second nature.

There are a small group of people who speak more slowly when they get nervous. However, for these presenters, the problem is again not really a slow delivery of words, but rather a slow delivery of ideas. These people tend to keep reiterating their ideas in the nervous belief that they haven't explained them properly the first time around. They are like the person who has to keep checking that they have locked the front door and turned the heating off. This problem also befalls people who haven't done a dry run of the presentation. The solution here is to prepare properly. Decide what you are going to say, say it, and then move on. With practise, and one or two rehearsals, this is easily achieved.

Pitch – Speaking in a monotone voice can kill even a very well-prepared talk. It is one of the most commonly cited faults of bad presentations. However, it is due to bad preparation, not bad delivery. How often do you have conversations with people and find yourself complaining about the flat inflection of their voice? We've all met people who have bored us, but this is usually down to what they choose to say, and not how they say it. We talk to people every day and there are times when what we hear annoys us, or upsets us, or shocks us, but you never find yourself saying something like: 'Yes, she has a point, but there's just no inflection in the way she says it.' In real life, intonation usually matches the content of what is being said.

Monotonic delivery is really a feature of presentations, not conversations. Something happens to some people when they go to speak before a group that flattens the intonation they would normally employ when communicating. What causes this to happen? Students are far more often guilty of this than practising professionals – looking at the difference between these two groups of speakers points to a possible reason why.

There are two main differences between students and professionals. The first is expertise. Where many of the students are unsteadily presenting a few months' part-time work to lecturers who are experts in the field, working professionals are talking about subjects, products or projects that they have been immersed in for years.

The second, and more telling, difference is the motivation of the two groups. The workers have a fixed goal in mind for their presentation: selling a product to a customer, persuading their boss to take a particular action, or simply helping their colleagues to do some aspect of their own jobs. The students do not have such a clear brief. They are presenting their work to their classmates, but this audience has no great need to hear about this work. In fact, they are making a presentation for the sake of making a presentation. It is just an exercise, not a functional communication.

In this situation, there is no practical need for the presentation except to give the students practise in presenting. Without a strong motive on the part of the presenter, the thinking seems to be: 'OK, I have to talk about this topic for this length of time, so I'll break down the material into a set of logical segments and each of these into a set of logical points, and then go through them one by one.' It is no wonder that the talk is delivered in a monotone; it is essentially a talk without feeling. The way to inject this feeling is to give the talk a narrative drive, to have it focused on achieving a particular goal. For this, there needs to be a clear motive for the presentation. It is also necessary that you speak with authority, so that you have a feeling of ownership of the ideas you are expressing.

The best way to inject life into your delivery is to simply know what you are talking about, have a reason to speak, and to believe in what you are saying. In the same way an actor will ask, 'What is my motivation for this part?' you must have a clear motive for your talk. Think about your audience and about what you want them to do as a result of listening to your presentation. Having this goal in mind will give a direction to your presentation, where each part of the talk leads them closer to this final goal. This will imbue your speaking style with a natural inflection.

Volume – This is really a fairly trivial problem. It is one thing that you can change quite easily without compromising your natural style. People's voices range widely in volume but it is rarely a problem when you speak too loudly. The problem is for people who don't speak loudly enough, and the solution is simple: speak up.

It may help to look frequently at the people at the back of the room. Apart from lengthening, and thus clearing, your chest and throat, by looking up, psychologically it will encourage you to pitch your words to them and this will lead you to speak louder. If the room is very big and there are a lot of people present, you will probably be given a microphone, or at least you should be, which relates to preparation, not delivery.

Guiding the Audience

Another way you can add texture to your verbal delivery, without altering your personal style, is to include sign-posting comments to remind the audience where you are. A document is laid out spatially, and when you pick it up, you can see immediately how it is divided up into chapters, sub-sections, paragraphs and even bullet points. However, a presentation is laid out temporally, it takes shape over time and the audience will need guidance on occasion about how you are progressing and where you are going next.

In conversation you do this all the time, inserting words and phrases that alert the listener to the meanderings your argument is taking. These are simple phrases such as:

however
then again
mind you
on the other hand
having said that
that said
but
nonetheless
nevertheless

The key to using phrases like these is not to deliberately script them into your presentation, but rather to believe strongly in what you are saying and allow yourself to say it with conviction. This will work the inflection into your speech automatically. People would far rather listen to a passionate speaker than a reserved one. If you have a clear aim for your talk and you have prepared thoroughly, you will be able to carry your argument with conviction, and you will use phrases like those listed above without thinking.

You may also include more deliberate points of inflection and reflection at the breaks between the larger segments of your talk. This kind of phrase stops the audience and says to them: 'Now let's think about where we are for a minute.' Some examples are:

interestingly
strangely enough
what strikes me here
what you may notice about this
you may be asking yourself
What do you think about that?
How do you react to this?
Does anything here strike you as unusual?
Why might we do such a thing?

Phrases like these alert the audience that something important has just taken place, or is about to take place. This technique of 'reacting to your own material' is something that you can deliberately script into your presentation. The more confidence you gain, the more comfortable you will feel about also adding pauses to enhance this technique.

Belief in what you are saying is the key driver to enhancing verbal inflection. Watch anyone in an argument. Assuming that they manage to keep control of their temper, their communication skills improve in several ways. Eye contact becomes fixed and often intense. All stuttering, mumbling and other signs of uncertainty usually disappear. Body language is heightened as hand gestures become exaggerated. And, most tellingly of all, verbal inflection becomes extremely pronounced. People really beat home their key points, even supplementing their verbal emphasis with gestures, such as pointing or banging a table in time with the words they are saying.

This process happens naturally and can, like so many of the other conversational skills we possess, be tapped into when making a presentation. Strong belief and a clear line of logic will bring colour and definition to the delivery of your words.

Verbal Tics

If you accept that your own natural conversational style is the best style you can adopt, then you realise that there is really no need for large amounts of demolition and reconstruction. With practise, it will become almost as natural as speaking to a friend. In other words, open-heart surgery is not required, merely regular exercise. However, for some people, some small, minor surgery may be needed. This is only local anaesthetic stuff, but the 'verbal tics' referred to here do require treatment.

To try:

In order to help you to put your ideas into words, it may be helpful to work with a colleague when preparing your presentation. Sit down together in an informal setting and first explain to your colleague in simple terms what the presentation is all about, who it is for, why you are giving it and what you intend to achieve. Then go through each of your sub-points, again explaining in your own words the logic behind each one.

This exercise will force you to treat your presentation as a logical story that builds to a sensible and useful conclusion. The supporting material (graphs, demonstrations, pictures) will then become subordinate to this narrative and the logic will flow more naturally. It will also give you practise in putting your ideas into words.

Figure 9.3. Phrases or gestures, if repeated, can become very noticeable, such as Mary Robinson's well-known hand gestures.

To try:

There is a very good exercise that you can use to improve your peripheral awareness when presenting. You will, however, need to get a group of like-minded people to meet at regular intervals. Write down a number of topics on small pieces of paper, fold them up and put them in an envelope. Each person in turn must pick out a piece of paper and speak on that topic for one or two minutes. The topics should be as obscure as possible: cats, golfing magazines, the history of Russia, how pencils work, lemonade, bell-jars, crown green bowling. Ideally, the group should be of a reasonable size, enough to make the speaker feel that he or she is making a presentation rather than chatting to a couple of friends.

This scenario would seem to go against one of the most important messages so far, namely the importance of excellent preparation, and indeed it does. However, the exercise does help you to get used to thinking on your feet. By making many of these short presentations, you are gaining the confidence to take your time and to think about what you are going to say next, even under the glower of an expectant audience. This can greatly accelerate your progress in becoming an accomplished presenter.

When using the term 'verbal tics', it should be pointed out that this only refers to the overuse of certain idioms and so maybe the term 'verbal bad habits' would be more appropriate. It is not being suggested that a stammer or a nervous twitch is something that can or should be tackled for the purposes of public speaking. In fact, when someone with a stammer makes a presentation, the audience very quickly adjusts to their style and pace of presenting and focuses on what they are saying and not how they are saying it. On the other hand, verbal bad habits are less ingrained in the manner of the speaker (and are thus more easily eliminated) but ironically, when left unchecked, they are far more distracting.

There are many examples of these bad habits, but some of the more common ones are:

and again
em
eh
basically
so to speak
as such
I mean to say
if you like
and then
as I said earlier

You may be thinking that phrases like these could act as space fillers in a similar way to the inflecting phrases looked at a few pages back. In other words, although they don't contribute any semantic meaning, they do help the speaker with the rhythm of the discourse, and when the speaker is thinking on his or her feet, this could be a help. Indeed, you would be right; a phrase like this doesn't add anything, but nor does it do any harm. In fact all presenters use phrases like these, especially 'em' and 'eh'. However, it does become a problem when such a phrase is used over and over again.

Many presenters have a crutch-word of choice and after a while it starts to dominate their presentation and the audience hear nothing else. The *em*s and *eh*s are not so serious and we all use these when we speak. An audience will usually filter them out in search of the useful information between these words. However, crutch words like 'basically' are much harder to conceal and can start to clutter your delivery.

It is not that difficult to remove these from your presentation, but it does take practise. You will first have to get a trusted colleague to tell you if you have any of these verbal bad habits because you probably won't notice them for yourself. Secondly, only focus on the really eccentric ones. A proliferation of *em*s and *eh*s, for example, is probably down to a hesitancy emanating from poor preparation and if you try too hard not to say these words, you will only make it harder to get on and deliver your message.

For the other words and phrases, awareness before the talk will push them closer to consciousness and you will hear them in your mind, and increasingly avoid saying them. The more times you present, the more you will notice other things around you and the more adept you will be at side-stepping the problem. This 'peripheral awareness', by the way, will also alert you when you are standing in front of the screen, fiddling with a pen or change in your pocket, or, worst of all, going over time.

Key points:

Use your own natural conversational style when presenting.

If you naturally speak quickly, don't try to speak slowly, but instead inject pauses into your delivery to allow the audience to digest each point.

Use guiding phrases to alert the audience to the natural divisions in your presentation.

10. ENERGY AND ENTHUSIASM

An engineer who was an expert in the area of heat treatment once gave a presentation in a somewhat eccentric style. He had a fairly dishevelled appearance, his speech was hurried – at times garbled – and he flailed his arms and moved about the room incessantly.

Figure 10.1. Enthusiasm is always engaging.

He began his talk in the most unusual way, spending the first few minutes describing the sword-makers of the middle ages whose job it was to make swords for the king's army. He spoke of how revered these people were, held in near mystical esteem because they were able to magically alter the properties of pieces of brittle iron into instruments of power. They could only do this with a deep understanding of material composition as well as the periods and temperatures of heating, holding and cooling. 'The subtlety of the sword-maker's art', he suggested, 'is no different from that of the heat treatment engineer of today: multiple factors, nonlinear relationships, interdependency of variables.'

All of the time this parallel was being drawn, you could see that the presenter had a genuine love and fascination for his subject. The opening analogy, although grand, was believable and the audience was carried into the presentation willingly. Although by no means polished, enthusiasm more than anything sold the presentation to the audience. Afterwards everyone spoke warmly about the presenter and the presentation that he had made.

The case for enthusiasm is easily stated: if you are not interested in what you are saying, how can you expect your audience to be? Enthusiasm is infectious. It is the one thing that can keep an audience interested even when the structure is a mess. (Of course, if the structure is a mess, then the presentation won't achieve anything.) Coupled with good preparation, the magic ingredient of enthusiasm can make for a mesmerising talk.

Figure 10.2. Strong personal belief is a powerful element in any presentation.

Even religious zealots in the street shouting about the sins of man and the end of the world can hold a strange grip on your attention. You will often find yourself stealing a look in their direction, careful not to make eye contact, drawn by the passion of the speaker. You might not agree with much, or indeed any, of what they say but something still makes you curious. It's almost as if you want to know why on earth that person is so driven; what inspires their enthusiasm?

Harnessing this Energy

Most readers will be able to relate to what has been said about enthusiasm so far. However, many of you will have thought: 'Yes, enthusiasm sells, but it's not really my natural style to present with that kind of energy,' or, 'OK, but how do you get enthusiastic about the kind of stuff that I have to present at work?' This is a fair point. Extreme cases have been depicted to suggest the infectious power of enthusiasm. You are not encouraged to try to ape the style of a Baptist preacher or a children's television presenter. Trying to force enthusiasm will make you come across as terribly false. There are, however, a number of principles regarding enthusiasm that might help you to harness its energy.

Don't be unenthusiastic – This may sound obvious but you will realise that this rule is often broken if it is paraphrased more succinctly as: never apologise. People often apologise when they are presenting. They apologise for slides that can't be read from the back of the room; for items that they didn't bring with them; for not being able to explain things very well; for not knowing as much as some of the people in the audience; for not being able to get the computer to work; they apologise at the start of the presentation to the people who will have heard all of this before and after the presentation for going over time.

Simply put, if there is something in your presentation that necessitates an apology, then it shouldn't be in your presentation. If your graphs cannot be seen properly from the back of the room, redraft them so that they can be seen. If the room is too big for everyone to be able to hear you, organise to have a microphone. If you're worried about having too much material, rehearse the presentation, and if it takes too long leave some of the material out.

By apologising, you are not only drawing attention to the weaknesses, you are also insulting the audience. You are saying to them: 'I could have done this properly, but I didn't. Sorry.' Not only is it insulting, it is also annoying. People come to hear you speak because they have a need that you, the expert, can satisfy. They want you to deliver, not mess around making excuses for not delivering. Like all conversations, a presentation is a collaborative process, two parties trying to work together to get to a shared goal. People in the audience are rarely there to shoot you down or to pick holes in your argument. They are there to learn something with your help. They are rooting for you.

So, stand up and deliver your talk emphatically. Believe in what you say and say it without apology. Don't second-guess yourself. In the end, the audience may decide that your presentation was not effective, but you shouldn't lead them to this conclusion yourself.

Boredom is relative – Often people say that there are some topics that are just plain boring, and it is impossible to breathe life into them with any amount of enthusiasm. However, like everything else relating to presentations, you can only discuss this in the context of a particular audience. So when someone refers to 'boring' material, you have to ask the question: 'Boring to whom?'

Is the weather forecast a boring television programme? It may be to some people, but if you are getting married, going sailing, or planning a barbecue, you'll probably find it quite engaging viewing. Your need will dictate how interesting you find something.

Your audience will have a keen interest in what you are going to talk about; if they didn't, then why would they come to listen to you? In some cases, the audience may not realise how important your material is to them, for example in the case of a sales pitch or a presentation about safety in the workplace. In instances like these, you have to explain the importance of what you are going to say to them first. But once you have done this, you should realise that there is a good reason for them to listen, and this should give you enthusiasm.

The audience have a need, which you are addressing. This may be boring to other people but it won't be boring to them. Realise this and respect their need. Assume that your talk is of the utmost importance and deliver it with conviction. If you do this, the audience will perceive an earnestness and an energy that will carry them along with you.

Figure 10.3. Often women will be bored listening to men talk about golf. But this woman is listening intently to a very detailed discourse on the subject because she has a need that this golf instructor is satisfying. Knowing that you are meeting a need of your audience is a good way to generate enthusiasm about any topic. Boredom, for an audience, is relative.

Get your story straight – This third principle relating to enthusiasm is coupled with the second. Once you have outlined your reason for presenting, you should then map out a clean line of logic by which you can reach this goal. This will give your presentation an arrow-like quality that

takes the audience right through from a clear introduction to a logical
conclusion. The more coherent this line of argument is in your own
head, the more strongly you will be able to deliver it to the audience.

Everyone has seen presenters who seemed slightly bored and listless;
this is usually because these presenters have not planned clearly where
they wish to go. The presentation does not have an aim to achieve something specific. This lack of a target saps the energy of delivery and it
becomes just a flat recitation of points. Instead, the presentation should
be an unfolding story, which will give it purpose and energy.

Personal conviction – This may not always be applicable, but very often
it is. The simplest way to inject enthusiasm into a presentation without
looking forced or false is to speak about something you feel strongly about
in the first place. Very often presentations you give at work involve you
summarising something you've done, or overseen other people doing,
and making recommendations based on this. The recommendations you
make are *your* recommendations. *You* have thought things through and
these are the conclusions *you* have reached.

This personal ownership of the ideas of a presentation can rouse
great energy. Obviously you don't want to let yourself get carried away,
but too often presenters rein in their personality to such an extent that
they distance themselves from what they are saying and this inevitably
makes the presentation dull.

*Figure 10.4. A strong belief in what you are saying – as usually occurs in an argument
– brings out your best communication skills. Eye contact, inflection of speech, and
body language all become pronounced without the speaker's conscious intervention.*

10. Energy and Enthusiasm

Remember the way communication skills are heightened in an argument. Eye contact becomes fixed and intense. All stuttering, mumbling and other signs of uncertainty usually disappear. Hand gestures become exaggerated, and verbal inflection becomes extremely pronounced. Assuming that this can all be kept under control, a good dose of personal conviction goes a long way towards boosting the energy of your delivery.

Key points

Don't apologise for any anything in your presentation.

Respect the audience's need, and deliver on this need with conviction.

I1. BODY LANGUAGE

One of the biggest red herrings when it comes to presentations is body language. Whole books are written on body language, but it is largely a non-issue for presenters. People have been led to believe that there is some subtle and secret code of the body that will make you utterly believable and fascinating to any audience. This is almost all rubbish.

Is it being suggested that body language is not part of how the presenter communicates? No. Is it being suggested that the way you say something (your tone of voice, as well as your physical manner) is not as important or even more important than the words you use? No. Certainly these things are important, in fact very important, but that is not to say that focusing explicitly on body language will be helpful.

A quiz question is sometimes posed: 'What is the cause of all human death?' The answer is: 'lack of oxygen to the brain'. The logic behind this answer is that death is pronounced when the brain is dead, and this happens when there is no longer enough oxygen delivered to this vital organ to sustain its function. So, if you have a heart attack, the heart stops pumping blood around the body, the blood brings oxygen to the brain, the brain stops functioning, and you die. Therefore, would it not be logical to conclude that if we wish to prevent death on the roads, or due to war or famine, the solution is simple: invent a device that keeps brains oxygenated so that people don't die?

This is, of course, absurd, but a similar argument is used in regard to body language. The signs that our bodies give off tell an audience that we are knowledgeable, confident, enthusiastic, honest; so if we learn enough about these signs we can have our audiences believe that we are any of these things. This is all very well, but have you ever tried to feign enthusiasm or confidence? Have you ever tried to control your own body language as you are speaking? This is akin to keeping your brain oxygenated at all times. It's looking at the immediate causes rather than the more deep-rooted ones.

Body language results naturally from how you feel about what you are doing. If you are honest in what you're saying, then you will look honest. If you are knowledgeable, you will look knowledgeable, by and large. You may have the odd distracting or even contradictory gesture, and as with verbal tics, you should get a trusted colleague to point these out to you so you can focus on eliminating them. But most of the time, body language complements what is being said. Why else, as animals, would we have evolved such a rich collection of behaviours if it didn't contribute to communication?

Our bodies speak all the time, and usually without our conscious intervention. Trying to control these movements directly and choreographing them into some dance that expresses a certain style is both extremely difficult and utterly unnecessary. Even the greatest actors don't attempt to control their body language directly. Rather they 'get into character'. They imagine the moods and emotions of the person they are playing and allow their bodies to move, as naturally as they can, with these emotions. There have been several famous, extreme examples of this, including Dustin Hoffman going for days without sleep to perfect the frazzled look for his role in *Marathon Man*.

So, although your demeanour is a symphony of subtle gestures and nuances, it is not one that it is very easy or wise to try to control. In the same way as with verbal style, it is far easier to simply believe in what you are saying. However, as with verbal style, there are a few things that you can tweak. The main points to remember are as follows.

Stand – Always stand up when you are giving a presentation. You have been asked to speak before a group and you should take this responsibility seriously. If it is a longer session involving questions and discussion, then it may be appropriate to sit down at a later stage but at least for your opening remarks you should be standing. Sitting down, quite simply, makes you look smaller and less important and so you are underselling yourself, particularly to a group that does not know you. Sitting down also curtails your movement (and therefore energy) and this is rarely a good thing.

Another important reason to stand up when you are presenting is to allow the audience to see you. In the same way that you should look at people when you are talking to them, people will want to look at you when they are listening. This is natural, and if you are hidden from view, it can be very frustrating for the audience. As well as this, you should try to avoid having obstacles between you and the audience. Don't stand behind a podium or a desk, and rearrange the layout of the room to suit your own needs.

Open gestures – One of the most well-known rules of body language is to avoid the hostile folded-arms gesture. The importance of this, and many other gestures like it, are probably blown out of all proportion. How often have you seen two women talking intently to each other with their arms folded across their chests? If you have put together an excellent and useful presentation the audience will not suddenly lose faith in everything you say if you momentarily fold your arms or shake your head.

That said, where possible, open gestures are better than closed ones. Don't fold your arms or cover your mouth. Don't hide behind the furniture in the room or cower below the screen. Stand square on to the audience with your hands loose and free, look them in the eye and try to be as friendly and open in your demeanour as possible. This is not to say that you should force a smile if it is not your natural pre-disposition to do so, but neither should you talk down to your audience, particularly when someone asks a question.

Hand movements – A woman once made a presentation at a course with her hands clasped very noticeably in front of her. She looked, for all the world, like an opera singer; she had precisely that stance with one hand above the other, fingers hooked. When asked about it later, she said that she had a tendency to move her arms around so she thought it better to keep them anchored together to prevent this as she was worried it might be distracting.

Figure 11.1. We have developed the use of hand gestures to accompany the words that we say. More often than not, these enhance communication and shouldn't be stifled.

Indeed, repeated hand gestures, just like repeated idioms of speech, can be distracting, but this is very rare. One example was where the speaker jerked his arm outwards repeatedly, as if he was constantly throwing something away, and the sheer incessancy of this movement meant that it came to dominate everyone's attention. But this is very much the exception and to say that hand gestures are distracting is like saying that facial expressions are distracting. In fact, they add inflection and emphasis to the words being spoken.

Most people move their hands all the time when they speak. It's a natural thing we have evolved for a good reason. Added to the variations of voice and facial expression, hand movements help to meter out the points we are making as we communicate. They give the audience visual clues about the breaks in our verbal delivery. Remember, unlike a written document, in a presentation the audience cannot easily see what's coming next. They can't glance over the page and see that they are coming to the end of a paragraph. Anything that helps them to do this, is good.

You may unconsciously do something that is distracting, like constantly tap your trouser pocket or fiddle with your glasses. It is important to get someone to observe one or two of your presentations and point any such habits out to you. When you become aware of these behaviours, with practise, you will quickly eliminate them. All other movements are a good thing, and should be left alone.

Don't fidget – There is a simple truism, often cited, regarding presentations: 'Don't compete with distractions, they will always be more interesting than you.' Although this sounds like a cynical reflection, it is undoubtedly true because listening, even for a keenly interested audience, is hard work. It involves nonstop concentration. The problem arises when a weary audience and a nervous presenter collide, and the presenter starts to fidget with something – a pen, guide notes, change, keys, a pointer, a demonstration prop – and this item comes to hypnotise the audience and they end up remembering nothing else from the presentation.

There is an easy solution to this problem and that is simply to leave any such distractions down when you are not using them. Again, you may need someone to point these things out to you, but when you realise what the distractions are, they are easily dealt with.

People holding guide notes can be particularly distracting. Although not as noisy as clicking pens, they are more visually arresting and it can look like the speaker is waving a flag in front of the audience. Don't present without guide notes, but it is better if you place them on the

Key points:

More often than not, your body language and the message you are communicating will complement each other.

Allow yourself to be seen by the audience.

Get a trusted colleague to alert you to any distracting actions that you may do when presenting.

desk beside you and refer to them when necessary, rather than holding them in your hand where they draw so much attention to themselves. Doing it this way will also force you to take short breaks between your different points, which is never a bad thing.

Movement – People are often advised to keep still when presenting, as to move around the room too much is distracting. This, however, is rarely the case, and the movement would need to be pretty extreme to really undermine the talk. Usually the opposite is true.

At one conference there was a long afternoon of 14 or 15 presentations, one after the other. Each speaker had their slides on a laptop, which projected an image many times their size on to a central screen, while the speaker stood off to one side in near-darkness behind a fairly large podium. One by one the speakers came to the podium, fired up their PowerPoint presentations, and spoke solemnly for the allotted time.

Then, towards the end of the session, one of the speakers did a remarkable thing. He walked from the podium, across the front of the screen, to the far side of the room, drew a sketch on a blackboard and turned to look at the audience as if to say, 'Do you get that?' and then walked back to the podium and continued to speak.

What made this most ordinary event remarkable was the fact that it was such a breath of fresh air compared to what all of the other speakers had done. It had been one talk after another, same style, large screen, bullets on slides, disembodied voice, 'any questions', 'thank you for your time' – every one the same. This speaker showed that he could move about and draw and write, and the effect of this humble bit of animation was remarkable.

If you move about, it gives your talk animation. You will not be beside your computer or guide notes at all times, but this can be good as it will force you to periodically return to these props, and this will add those all important little breaks between your main points. Most people speak faster when they present, so keeping the pace of your talk in check in this way is helpful. You should, of course, try to remain visible at all times, but movement will probably help in this regard as there is rarely a single place in the room where everyone can see you. Repeated rhythmic movements, such as swaying, are a distraction but general movement about the room will add colour to your talk.

12. NERVES

Everyone gets nervous when they have to speak before a group. Many people get very nervous, and for some, the prospect is so intimidating that they avoid making presentations altogether. The issue of nerves is the single biggest preoccupation of people when they make presentations, and yet, the only way to deal with them is to avoid dealing with them entirely.

Dealing with Nerves

There is a simple cure for nerves and that is to get on with it. Don't worry about them or try to remedy them directly: just prepare well, stand up and say what you have to say.

Imagine you are studying for an important exam. There is no doubt that doing exams is an extremely stressful business. You need to be able to represent a large amount of knowledge in just a few hours, and there may be a life-changing outcome riding on the result. So, in the hours and days leading up to important exams, people get nervous.

What do you do about these nerves? You work as hard as you can to do well in the exam. The question is rarely posed, 'How does one avoid the nerves of doing exams?' This is a case where the way to deal with them is to simply deal with the source of the nerves – fear of doing badly in the exam – and the same can be said of making a presentation.

Nerves are a symptom of a problem, and the way to deal with the nerves is to tackle that problem. If someone is taken into hospital in terrible pain, the doctors in the hospital will try to find out, as quickly as they can, what is causing this pain. They may give the patient a pain-killer, but if the patient starts to feel better as a result, he or she will not simply be discharged. The question still remains: What caused the pain and how can we deal with this problem? Nerves are like pain, the body's reaction to a problem. Unfortunately there are no painkillers for nerves (or rather, none that won't compromise your delivery), so it is even more important to tackle the root-cause of these nerves.

There are two ways to approach this problem. The first is to make sure that none of the things that can go wrong do, by means of excellent and thorough preparation. The second thing is to practise. Giving presentations is something that many people have hardly ever done. It takes practice to get used to the feeling of being in front of a group and hearing the sound of your own voice. With each presentation you give,

To try:

One of the main sources of nerves is the fear of the unknown. One way to reduce these nerves is to quality-assure as many aspects of your presentation as possible. Make a list of all of the things you have to bring with you (notes, computer, demonstrations, acetates, handouts) as well as all of the things you have to do (check the overhead projector, check the room, contact members of the audience) and tick off each item as you account for it. Also, for everything that can go wrong, make sure you have a backup where this is feasible. For example, bring your slides on disc as well as on your laptop. Bring overhead acetates as well as your soft copy. Bring extra whiteboard pens in case the pens supplied don't work, and so on.

the feeling of strangeness will diminish and you will fear these situations less and less.

The Benefits of Nerves

So, the more times you present, and the better prepared you are each time, the less nervous you will feel. But will you ever get to the stage where you don't feel nervous at all? The answer is: probably not. Even the most experienced speakers will tell you that they get a bit nervous before any talk, but be assured, this is a good thing. Nerves prod you in to asking questions about your preparation and they give you extra energy when you speak.

Figure 12.1. Nerves enhance performance by making you think more quickly, ask more questions about your preparation, and by giving you energy in advance.

In this way, sometimes the most nervous speakers make the best presentations. Their aim is to make the presentation as painless and as quick as they can, for both themselves and the audience, and this very often leads to a concise and polished talk.

When faced with a difficult topic and a large group to present to, one speaker who was very nervous used this energy to drive her talk positively. She stood up, outlined a clear line of logic for what she was going to present and why this would be important, went through each of her key points, referring to a handful of clear diagrams and pictures, came briskly to a conclusion, politely answered a few questions, and then sat down. It was short, clear and to the point; a presentation with no fat on it whatsoever. Her nerves had made her to think critically about what she was doing and this led her to prepare an effective, as well as brief, presentation.

Nerves Are Invisible

We all dwell in an inner world that is full of emotions, dreams and memories. At any waking second of the day, we could be planning a job at work, dreaming of a holiday, worrying about the health of a family member, remembering a funny story or trying to solve a problem. However, the people around us are not aware of any of this. Think about when you walk down a crowded street, and think of all of the people that you pass, all of those faces, and behind each one a set of dramas and ideas as complex as your own. But to you they just look like the passive faces of ordinary people busily making their way.

Figure 12.2. You may feel nervous, but this rarely shows on the surface. People are very good at hiding their true emotions.

So it is in presentations. Think of all of the presentations you have gone to. Some were engaging, some dull, some confusing; some went on too long; some were fascinating. You sat there and listened, but how often did you think about the hassles the presenter had in putting the talk together, or the sleepless night that preceded it?

Key points:

Don't focus on nerves, focus on the job of presenting.

The audience won't notice your nerves.

In general, nerves improve performance.

People are often surprised to learn that other presenters who have spoken in the same set of presentations as they have were just as nervous as they were. Simply put: nerves are invisible. When someone gets up to speak, you listen to what they have to say and this becomes your focus, not how nervous they may be.

It has been said that learning to present is like learning to drive. The first time you do it, it is like changing gears in a car, there is too much to do at one time. However, with practise, it becomes second nature. The aim is to present to a group with the same ease with which you would talk to a friend. The only way to do this is to practise until presenting becomes something you are used to doing. When you get to this stage, you will be able to focus more on what you are trying to explain than on the basic task of getting your sentences out in one piece and keeping an eye on your guide notes. Again, it is just like learning to drive. Once you have become used to changing gears and turning corners without huge effort, you can then start to think about where you are going. The exercise described earlier will help to accelerate this learning process.

PART FOUR: BRIDGING THE GAP

So far, the task of making a presentation has been approached in a very general way. The issues that have been explored up to this point relate pretty much to any presentation, given by any speaker, to any audience. In all such cases, it is necessary to know your audience, decide on a clear aim, structure your material, use your conversational skills to deliver the talk, maintain audience contact and believe in what you are saying. *All* points apply to *all* presentations. However, this part will deal specifically with bridging the gap between the presenter's expert knowledge and the knowledge of the audience.

The aim here is to understand a little bit about what makes the penny drop. When you say, 'Ah yes, I've got that now,' what change has taken place in your mind? Understanding this process and explaining complex ideas is an important part of presenting, and yet very little study has been done and little has been written about this process.

The ideas in this part of the book are not just aimed at engineers, or scientists, doctors, accountants, mathematicians, psychologists, architects or lawyers. All presentations involve the bridging of some gap between what is simple to the presenter, and what is new and strange to the audience. The communication principles here apply to all presentations – again, you already use these tools in conversation, but they are too seldom employed when presenting.

13. MENTAL BRIDGING

The communication task can be summarised as taking what's in the mind of the presenter and putting it into the minds of the audience. In order to tackle this problem, then, it may help to have a quick look at how ideas are stored in the mind. To demonstrate this, write down the answer to each of the following:

1. How many sides does a hexagon have?
2. How many windows are there in your house?
3. What is your most impressive physical skill?
4. What event most stands out in your memory of the first day of your current job?

The answer to the first question is six, and there is only one right answer. You either know this answer or you don't, and knowledge of this kind is what psychologists call *propositional knowledge.* In simple terms, propositional knowledge is a series of facts, and they can be manipulated by logical operations to infer other facts. For example, if you know that Paris is in France, and that John was born in Paris, then you can infer that John is French. This kind of logic, not always so simple, can be used to construct elaborate theories and formulae that can then be made to do all sorts of useful things. In most formal professional education, the learning of propositional knowledge, and how to manipulate it dominates.

However, this is by no means the only way that your brain can store knowledge, as can be seen by looking at the answers to the other questions. When referring to how ideas are stored in our minds, cognitive psychologists favour the term *mental representations.* The propositions just examined (a hexagon has six sides, John is French) are only one type of mental representation. The second question elicits quite a different type. It is probable that you didn't know the answer instantly. And yet, despite the delay, it is also probable that you got the correct answer in the end.

To figure out how many windows are in your house, you probably took a mental tour and counted all of the windows that you could see in your mind's eye. (Interestingly, most people take a tour around the outside of their house, whereas some walk around the inside of the house. There's no obvious reason for this difference.)

If you have recently bought new windows or curtains, you probably knew the answer to this question in the form of a proposition, and were able to answer it instantly. But for most people, the answer is only generated by having recourse to another form of mental representation. This type of *knowing* is like a virtual reality tour of a space you are familiar with. The dimensions will not be accurate but the general layout will be, and could, for example, help you to navigate your way around your own house in the dark, at least better than a stranger would. It is also detailed enough to enable you to count the number of windows. The mental picture is a good deal richer than any set of statements that could be used to describe it. It is this, of course, that makes seeing a picture or a demonstration so much more satisfying and useful than just hearing about it.

The third question is something different entirely. Psychologists refer to our ability to do things physically as *procedural knowledge*. Such tasks often don't require any conscious understanding of what is going on (for example, your knowledge of how to ride a bicycle cannot be put into words in the same way as your knowledge of the words of a song) but they still represent a type of knowing, and it is a knowing that cannot be reduced to a set of definitions or mathematical equations.

The fourth question, about the first day in your current job, delves into yet another type of mental representation. Psychologists usually refer to memories such as those of your first day at work as *episodic memories*. This is the memory of events and we all store a great many of these. We sort, retrieve and communicate these episodic memories by means of stories. Some people would say that a story is just a set of propositions but this is a gross simplification. Ask a few friends to tell you the story of Goldilocks and you will see that there is a great variety in the length and details of the stories told, but they will still all be recognisable as the same story.

There is something central to any story (the point, or the moral), something around which the details arrange themselves to form a coherent whole. Often the central point that inspires the story is an emotion or a mental picture that is very difficult, in itself, to put into words. And the boundaries of the story can be easily moved. You could seek a different pattern from the same life events quite easily. An episodic memory is far too complex to be considered as a single, unique set of propositions. The stories that are spun from these episodes are an extremely powerful communication tool, which is under-utilised by most presenters.

These are only some of the different types of mental representation. So trying to understand what goes on in your mind when you say that you understand something could turn out to be quite difficult. In addition to this, there is a great deal of debate among psychologists about how these categories of mental representation should be divided. The divisions, as they have been presented above, are in no way absolute. And even the idea of a logical proposition that seems to be straightforward, is not always clear-cut when you look into it.

Figure 13.1. How do you take complex knowledge and most efficiently transfer it into the mind of someone else who needs to use it?

The good news is that the complexity and richness of mental representations in no way impedes our communication effort. There is a simple solution and it operates as follows:

- I have a complex mental representation of an idea in my head.
- I wish to transfer it into your head.
- I can't easily break down this representation into its component parts because I don't know enough about how the mind does this very sophisticated job.
- So, rather than trying to construct the mental representation from scratch, I will instead compare it to another – similarly rich – mental representation that is already established in your own brain.

The easiest way to demonstrate this process at work is with an example. Pick up any Sunday newspaper magazine and look through it.

There will almost certainly be a feature on wine. Each week, there will be a 'bottle of the week' and maybe an article on a particular wine region or wine-grower. This poses a communication challenge: How do you describe the taste of wine? There are remarkably few words to describe taste: sweet, sour, bitter and salty are the only obvious ones. Other words, such as intense, long, clean, complex and rich only describe the degree of taste. There are a great many words to describe, for example, an object's appearance – several hundred words for colour alone – but very few to describe the taste.

The mental representations we have for taste, however, are complex. We can discern and remember very subtle differences in flavour, but we only have a handful of words with which to express these sensations. The answer is to relate a new complex taste-representation to a complex taste-representation that has already been formed. You may not have tasted a particular wine before, but if you have tasted sour apples, then you may have a good idea of what it will be like. And this opens the door to the rich analogical lexicon of the wine writer, who can now compare wine to: any fruit, honey, caramel, butterscotch, vanilla, dark chocolate, tobacco, petrol, wet slate, nettles, nuts and tea. On top of these analogies are a whole family of new words used solely to describe wine. Again it is important to realise that these are not absolute terms; they only work if you have experienced the taste of the thing you are comparing with, and have formed the necessary complex mental representations.

Figure 13.2. Descriptions of the taste of wine (or the taste of anything, for that matter) can only be achieved by analogy with the taste of something else. It is almost impossible to describe these from first principles.

The same kind of links can be formed for all complex mental representations. The audience already have the building blocks with which you can most expediently make your point. The concepts of functions, graphs, mathematical models, equations, processes and systems are all second-nature to an engineer or scientist, for example, but would be baffling to someone from a non-technical background. Accountants talk about equity, accruals, materiality, futures, control deficiency, favourable variance, imputed interest and due diligence. Medics refer to case history, PERL, CPR, ECG, triage, pathology, toxicology, epidemiology and dyspnoea. We use the terms relevant to our own field without realising how rich in meaning they are. With imagination and effort, it is possible to think up of all sorts of analogies and examples to bring theoretical ideas to life.

The overall point here is that if in a presentation you wish to take a concept and effectively reconstruct it in the minds of the audience, then a very efficient way to do this is to compare that concept with an already-formed concept that the audience is already in possession of. Trying to construct that concept from first principles is much harder to do.

This is not, for a moment, to suggest that a presentation should be general and vague and contain little technical content. The analogies and examples that link already-formed mental representations to new ones don't replace hard theory, they simply assist in explaining it. It has been too often the case in the education of technical subjects to rely solely on mathematical derivations to establish theories. The thinking seems to be: 'In order to teach this, I must establish the theory first. By deriving theory, I have effectively explained the theory.' This is not the case. As will be seen in the next section, without the linking of mental representations, comprehending abstract theory is unnecessarily hard work.

Psychological Perspective

The idea that the explanation of general theory can be greatly enhanced by the inclusion of a link to a tangible, already-formed, mental representation should not surprise too many readers, who have surely seen examples and analogies used to good effect. And yet, many presenters don't take the time to include these tools in their talks. To encourage you to do so, it may help to look at the psychological rationale behind this way of communicating. Consider the following problem:

Suppose that you have four cards. There is a number on one side of each card and a letter on the other. The four cards are set on a table with the following sides face up:

A	4	K	7

The letter-number pair on each card obeys the following rule:

If there is a vowel on one side of the card then there must be an odd number on the other side.

The question now posed is this: which of the above cards would you have to turn over to determine if this rule has been followed? You might like to think about this for a minute.

The answer is that you must turn over the A and the 4. Most people get the A. It is a vowel so you must see the reverse side of the card to see if the vowel is coupled with an odd number. However, many people don't pick the 4. If there were a vowel on the other side of this card, then the rule would have been broken. The reason that people often make this mistake is that the rule seems to concern vowels and odd numbers and they therefore disregard the even number 4. However, an even more common mistake that people make is to pick the 7. The thinking here is, 'Vowels must be followed by odd numbers, so we must see if there is indeed a vowel on the other side.' However, the rule states, 'If there is a vowel then there must be an odd number.' It does not state the reverse, 'If there is an odd number then there must be a vowel.'

Even people with a strong mathematical bent tend to get this wrong. This kind of logical juggling is very difficult, but if the problem is presented in another way, it becomes a lot simpler.

Suppose you own a clothes shop. You have told your cashiers that they must sign the back of any receipt for a transaction in excess of €50. At the end of the day, you are working out the takings for the day and making sure that all of the receipts are in order. One of your cashiers is dealing with a customer. You notice four receipts on the counter beside him. Two are face up and two are face down. Of the two that are face up, one is for a transaction of €15 and the other for a transaction of €380. Of the two that are face down on the table, one is signed by the cashier and the other is not. Which of the four receipts would you turn over to see if your directions had been followed?

It probably doesn't take too much mental effort to come up with the answer to this problem. You would have to turn over the unsigned receipt to see if it were for a transaction greater than €50. You would also have to turn over the €380 receipt to see if the back had been signed. There is an exact mapping between this problem and the earlier one as follows:

A – €380 receipt
4 – unsigned receipt
K – €15 receipt
7 – signed receipt

Why was the abstract problem so difficult while the equivalent problem based on a real-life scenario was quite simple? This experiment, first carried out by Wason and Johnson-Laird in the early 1970s, has been the subject of much discussion over the years. The interpretation is particularly useful for us here. It is based around the demands that the two problems place on memory.

Memory can be split into two main groups: long-term memory, and short-term or working memory. Working memory is what we use when we receive new information. It is like a scratch-pad in your mind, where new items are juggled while we try to make sense of them and eventually encode them into long-term memory. In long-term memory, items that have been understood and rehearsed remain, and can do so without being forgotten for years or even decades.

If the problem is totally abstract (i.e. couched in terms of A-4-K-7), we must use working memory to juggle the various abstract quantities in order to come up with a solution. This is hard work. We can only retain several items in working memory at any one time. On the other hand, the receipts scenario makes its demands on long-term, not working memory. The shop-receipts scenario, however, is easy to identify with. It is what is known as a *permission schema*. It can be paraphrased logically as follows:

> *If activity X is permitted only to people with property Y, then anyone doing X must have property Y.*

The abstract form of the problem made this rule hard to spot, but in the real version it was obvious. Another real scenario that works on the same premise is the consumption of alcohol in a bar. The logic runs like this: If you are drinking alcohol in a bar then you must be over 18 (card A above), but if you are in a bar and are over 18, it doesn't mean that you have to drink alcohol (card 7 above).

It would seem that we base a lot of our judgments, not on a logical analysis of the situation, but on a schematic basis, in other words on the basis of finding a match with a familiar schema we've seen before. Instead of having a small family of logical operations and applying them to a large number of similar situations, we instead learn to recognise many different logically identical scenarios and store these in long-term memory. When asked to understand a situation, we thus look for a match in memory and reason based on this.

On the face of it, this method of reasoning might seem cumbersome, but it is in fact very efficient given the way memory works. To figure things out with abstract logic requires working memory, which is very limited, whereas finding a match with something we have previously experienced and stored in long-term memory (schematic reasoning) is relatively easy as we are able to store many millions of facts and experiences without much effort.

The implication of all of this for making a presentation is simply: make your ideas real. Use analogies and examples to mentally bridge from your new ideas to what the audience already knows. In addition, demonstrations and stories can be used to make concepts more tangible and thus easier to understand and remember. The following chapters explore each of these four communication tools in more detail.

14. ANALOGIES

The recent invasion of Iraq was viewed by many in the United States as another potential 'Vietnam'. In the months following the fall of the old regime, efforts were made to form a 'Marshal plan' to effect an expedient withdrawal. The proponents of the invasion saw Saddam as 'Hitler'; they saw Kofi Annan and Jacques Chirac as the 'heirs of Neville Chamberlain'; and they viewed the seizing of Baghdad as the 'liberation of Paris'. However, those who opposed the war suggested that Bush and his cabinet were manipulating the facts the way Lyndon Johnson had done at the 'Gulf of Tonkin'; they had been determined to control a foreign power in the pursuit of a new kind of 'domino theory'; and that the invasion of Baghdad was redolent of 'Stalingrad'.

Analogies like these abound in politics and are usually used rhetorically. Although they do form a fast mapping between source and target, they can sometimes be dubious, largely because the Vietnam War, for example, is a fairly vast entity to use as a simple comparison with anything. However, in a more concise field, these connections can work wonders in a long and difficult presentation.

In this way the concept of electrical current can be likened to the flow of water, the scheduling of messages in a modern phone system can be likened to cars sharing the same lane on a motorway, the human body can be likened to an engine, the earth's atmosphere can be likened to a greenhouse, and a disease can be likened to an army.

Figure 14.1. One of the most commonly used analogies in physics is that between the flow of electricity and the flow of water.

There is no need to explore these analogies in detail. They are relevant only to the particular target audience in each case. Everyone reading this can, with a bit of thought, generate many analogies for their own purposes. Most often, the problem is not to help people think up useful analogies, but rather to get them to see the importance of doing so in the first place.

There seems to be what can only be labelled 'expert apathy' when it comes to the use of analogies. This goes right to the heart of why many presentations fail. The expert has a rich background against which to present his ideas, and it can be hard to put himself into the audience's shoes and imagine what it would be like to view the same material without this background.

For example, this book was typed on a computer, and the world of the computer interface is second nature to anyone who writes regularly. The concepts of application windows, file and directory storage, drag-and-drop graphics, pull-down menus and application icons are all well practised and well understood. You work in this environment without thinking for a moment about these things, in the same way that when you reach across the table to pick something up, you are not aware of the movements of your forearm and the manipulation of each finger, you are just picking something up. However, if you have ever had to teach someone about the computer environment from scratch (parents who grew up before the digital age, for example), then you realise how many of these concepts you have long been able to take for granted as you focus on the higher-level task you are engaged in.

Presenters underestimate the need for analogies to bridge these gaps. And while a confused and technologically alienated parent will stop you to tell you that you are not explaining yourself at all clearly, an audience at a presentation generally won't. They will sit quietly and you will have little idea that you have failed them.

An insight into why this happens is provided by work done on analogies by Kevin Dunbar in McGill University. Dunbar has studied the reasoning processes of scientists as they carry out their work. His research team has videotaped and audio-taped leading molecular biologists and immunologists as they reason and communicate in their weekly laboratory meetings. These scientists were discussing research findings: analysing data, formulating theories and designing experiments. Dunbar and his team analysed these meetings sentence by sentence and noticed some interesting things in relation to the use of analogy.

Firstly, analogical thinking is a key component of all scientific reasoning, with anywhere from two to 14 analogies used in each of the laboratory meetings studied. Secondly, these analogies were based on deep structural features. In other words, the analogies weren't just connecting superficial features in the communication process, they were doing real work. And thirdly, and most importantly, the tentative analogies that researchers formed to explain findings at the meetings were largely forgotten several months later, although the final findings of the experiments were remembered. It was as if the analogies were being used when bridging to a new mental representation, but when this new representation became firmly established, they were forgotten. Dunbar himself commented, 'The scientists appear to be using the analogies as scaffolding. Once they serve their purpose of building new explanations, they are discarded.'

Presenters, who are expert in their subject, don't often see the need for this kind of bridging. They understand what they are talking about. However, the audience is feeling their way in the dark and will benefit from such bridging analogies. In fact, in their absence, they will attempt to form analogies of their own, prompting such questions as, 'Is this like…?' and 'Would this be the same as?'

Learning is really a process of using analogies to form temporary platforms in the mind until they become solid, and then further analogies can be formed to bridge to the next concept, and so on. When young children are being taught multiplication, the concept is built up as an analogy with addition. Division is then taught, not usually by analogy with subtraction, but by analogy with multiplication, as a sort of reverse-multiplication process. However, when these new concepts become solid, there is no longer a need to relate them to previous analogical levels.

Looking again at the computer interface, the same process is at work. If you wish to move text from one location to another, then you use the 'cut and paste' commands on the computer. The first few times you carried out this task you very deliberately did the 'cut' action and then the 'paste' action. With practise, however, you don't even think about cutting or pasting, you simply think: 'I need to move this text to the start of this section,' and the actions to do this would be totally ingrained. When presenting you have to force yourself to go back to the mindset you had when the ideas weren't established, and help the audience to form these new tentative connections for the first time.

The computer interface is itself rich in analogy. Documents are called 'files' and are stored in 'folders'. If you wish to discard a file, you place it into the 'bin'. If this operation takes longer than a few seconds a small 'hourglass' appears to indicate that you may have to wait. If something then goes wrong, you may wish to check the 'control panel' to see if the computer is operating correctly.

These analogical references make the various terms more intuitively meaningful to a beginner. When you become expert, these references become just terms for actions that you understand and need not consciously think about.

Guidelines for Using Analogies

As suggested earlier, it would make little sense to give examples of analogies in detail, as they can only be judged in the context of a particular presentation task with a particular audience. However, it might be useful to list a few general guidelines regarding their use.

Accuracy – You will lose credibility very swiftly if you form an analogy that is fundamentally unsound: take, for example, a student who was chosen to take part in a presentation-skills competition. He formed an analogy to explain how glass-fibre composites work. This material, better known to most of us as fibreglass, has a very good combination of structural properties because of how it is made. Small glass fibres are held in a plastic substrate, so you get the toughness of a plastic combined with the hardness of glass.

The student in question opened by taking a packet of nuts out of one of his pockets and a bar of plain chocolate out of another. He then asked what you get when you bring these two together, at which point he produced a bar of whole-nut chocolate, explaining, triumphantly, that the combination was so much better than the two ingredients alone. The judges were stunned. What was this supposed to tell them, that when you mix nuts and chocolate you get nut-chocolate? Besides which, the inclusion of nuts doesn't make the chocolate bar any stronger (in fact it makes it weaker), so the analogy was woolly and trite and only turned the audience against the presenter.

In fairness, this should never really happen because a presenter will be a genuine expert on the topic in the way a student probably won't be. One of the features of expertise is the ability to see the connections between items in your field. While a novice only sees facts and details, the expert sees the pattern that brings these fragments together. With this ability to see connections, the presenter should be able to form credible and accurate analogies with ease. All it takes is a bit of imagination and effort.

Familiarity – An analogy maps a source analogue (what is known) to a target analogue (what is unfamiliar and needs to be explained). It may be stating the obvious, but you should make sure that the source analogue is indeed familiar to the audience. There is a well-known analogy in mechanics that maps the laws that govern vibrating mechanical systems (such as car suspensions) to the laws that govern DC electrical transients. Great play of this mapping is made in most mechanics books, but is this useful? Most students find mechanics difficult, so an analogy might be very welcome, but most students find DC transients even more difficult. Being told the friction in a mechanical system is analogous to the resistance in an electrical circuit may have some explanatory merit, but being told that the mass of the same mechanical system is analogous to the inductance of an electrical circuit is not necessarily so useful. This analogy, although a perfect and rich mapping between two complex areas, does not take the user anywhere useful. Some of the wine analogies from earlier are also misguided in this way. Knowing that a particular wine is going to taste like damsons is not much use to many people.

The more generally familiar an analogy is, the more people it will work for. You may have to be a bit more imaginative in thinking up a universal analogy but it will be worth it. However, you don't always have to map from a very general scenario, if you know your audience.

Know the audience's basic-level associations – If asked to name the two items in Figure 14.2, you would probably say, 'One is an apple and the other is a banana.'

Figure 14.2. How would you describe these objects? No doubt you would say 'apple' and 'banana', but this involves a choice of how much detail you go into when categorising an object. This can have important consequences when forming analogies.

To try:

When thinking of good analogies, you have to think outside of your normal frame of reference. The trick is: first be creative, then be critical.

Pick out the two or three most difficult concepts to explain in your talk. Take a few minutes to brainstorm ideas for analogies that could explain these concepts. At this stage anything goes. Come up with as many novel and far-reaching analogies as you can. When this is done, you can then start interrogating each idea critically to see if it holds water. You should only use analogies that are robust, otherwise you will undermine your credibility. If you go through this process, it's a certainty that you will be left with several, possibly invaluable, analogies that will greatly enhance your presentation.

There is nothing too remarkable about this, you might think, however, you have made a profound decision in how you chose to answer the question. You could have said, 'That is a picture of two types of fruit,' or, 'That is a Cox apple and that is a Burro banana.' Why did you pick 'apple' and 'banana' as being the right level of description?

Psychologists call the level at which you categorise something your *basic level association*. The brain judges this level according to what is pragmatic. On the one hand you need categories to be discriminating; on the other you don't want them to be so detailed as to burden memory by allowing unnecessary distinctions. Apples are round, green or red, hard and have pips. Bananas are long, yellow, soft and don't have pips. There are several easy categories that discriminate between the two items to a degree that is useful.

The point about base-level associations is that they vary from audience to audience. A conference of apple-growers will be *au fait* with the differences between a Cox's Orange Pippin and a Bramley. But you must be aware of whether you have to slide up or down the scale of associations. Where this becomes really important is in the case of using jargon and acronyms. Many audiences have been utterly baffled and alienated by sentences such as, 'The SL200 has a host unit and two S3 remote evaps with three fans on each coil.' Be extremely careful: you should check every single specialised term before your presentation and ask if it will be familiar to the audience. If there is any doubt, you should introduce it clearly when you mention it for the first time.

Loose jargon is far more damaging than you might think. It's not just the case that a small piece of your talk will be ineffective. The term in question may be pivotal If the audience spend the rest of the talk wondering what you meant by 'host unit' or what an 'SL200' is, then you will have broken the chain of logic of the whole presentation.

It should be pointed out, however, that it is possible to go to the other extreme as well. Many presenters are overly specific. They explain everything from first principles, failing to harness the swift shorthand of analogies. For example, the jargon-rich sentence included above makes perfect sense to some people. These terms (coil, SL200, S3, evap) act as a very useful shorthand for certain audiences. Analogies allow you to quick-step through many complex ideas by working with the pre-existing knowledge of the audience. This, once again, points to the importance of knowing your audience as well as you possibly can.

Use analogies in the introduction – Introductions were looked at in considerable detail earlier. It was then stressed that the audience needs to have a clear notion of where they are going from the start. Without this context, there is nothing to glue the individual items of the presentation together into something meaningful. So, if you have a good analogy that explains an important central concept to the audience, share it with them at the start.

This may sound obvious, but quite often presenters do the exact opposite. They work through the theory, the facts, the lists, the bullets, the graphs; then right at the end say something like, 'Now, as a final point it might be interesting to look at all of this from a different angle.' You should never try to surprise an audience in the last minute of a presentation. If you do, it might be too little, too late.

In conclusion, analogies allow a fast and extremely effective mapping between an audience's pre-existing knowledge and a new idea. They are a very efficient communication tool. The better you know your audience, the better you will be able to choose these analogies. It can take a bit of imagination, so a five- or 10-minute brainstorming session with a colleague will, as in so many other aspects, benefit your presentation greatly. And lastly, don't be afraid to be imaginative. An analogy is a bonus in your talk. If it works well, it will be greatly appreciated by the audience and it will make your talk more interesting, more effective and more memorable.

Key points:

Analogies that seem simple and unimportant to an expert presenter can be invaluable to a non-expert audience.

An inaccurate or trite analogy will undermine your credibility.

In order to form useful analogies, it is vital you know your audience.

15. EXAMPLES

There are two magic words that always enhance a presentation. Utter these two words and watch the gnarled expressions of a confused audience lighten. Sprinkle your presentation with these magical words to gently rouse the sleepers to life. What are the two words in question? 'For example'.

Examples bring abstract ideas to life. They make them real and easier to understand. You are meandering your way through a complex argument or idea and the audience is sitting there asking questions to themselves, 'What does she mean?' 'Can he justify this?' 'Can she clarify?' Then you utter the magic words and everyone relaxes, knowing that you will now make things clear.

Again, as with analogies, this does not mean you need to do away with abstract definitions or the mathematical equations that follow them. The example doesn't replace the theory, it assists it. However, the example links to a mental representation that is already formed through everyday experience, and this is a very neat communication trick.

Examples are never hard to find. It is, after all, the real-life application of a theory that makes the theory worth studying in the first place. There will always be several examples to choose from, so it might be useful to lay down a few guidelines in the best use of examples.

Spectacular examples – In a talk on the mechanical concept of resonance (the same process by which opera singers can shatter glass by singing at its natural ringing frequency), one of the examples used was the collapse of the Tacoma Narrows Bridge in November 1940 (Figure 15.1). Wind blowing across the span of the bridge was generating pulsating eddies that happened to be at the natural twisting frequency of the bridge. On the fateful day, the wind was persistently blowing at the critical speed, setting up a violent twisting motion that got more and more severe until eventually the bridge collapsed.

An example like this works in two ways. Obviously it grabs attention. Also, many people in the audience may have seen or heard of this before which, although diminishing the wow-factor somewhat, makes for a much better mental association. They are more likely to have a rich mental representation of something spectacular and famous than something obscure. This makes the mapping of theory to practical example easier.

Figure 15.1. A spectacular example not only grabs attention but is also likely to be familiar to your audience, thus making for a richer mental association. The collapse of the Tacoma Narrows Bridge is one of the most famous examples of resonance.

It is not being said that your examples should all be shocking and profound. First and foremost they have to be relevant and you are not encouraged to simply startle people at every turn. But if you do have a choice of examples to use, try to use those that will be most interesting and remarkable for your audience.

It might be that you work for an accounting firm and you are making a presentation to staff to explain the benefits of your new customer database. You need to choose one of your customers as a case study to show what the system can do. Going by the 'spectacular' principle as it has been described, it would be a good idea to pick the client that most people are familiar with, or the highest-profile client that you have, or the client that has been involved in a wrangle with your company over an issue addressed by this system, or simply the client whom most people in the room would have had direct dealings with. The term 'spectacular', like many of the terms used in this book, is relative to the audience each time.

Familiar examples – This might seem like a direct contradiction of what has been said in the previous point, but it is not. In fact it is precisely the same thing but in a different form. The spectacular examples mentioned in the last section work in part because, due to their high profile, they are already familiar to the audience. The same is obviously true of familiar examples: things from everyday life that most people would be intimately aware of.

In this regard, the opera singer shattering the glass is a good choice of example as it is well known, and will already have formed a rich mental representation in the minds of the audience, which you can then build on.

Figure 15.2 shows some examples that have been used. In one presentation on fluid pressures, the example of how the widget in a can of beer is used to generate a perfect pint of draught stout was used. Another talk on market competition focused on the pricing battle between mobile phone companies. This worked because it was certain that nearly everyone in the audience owned a mobile phone. And the humble golf ball was used to good effect in a presentation on the very difficult topic of 'boundary layer separation and drag' of fluids, the question posed (and answered), being 'Why do golf balls have dimples?' The example greatly helped.

Figure 15.2. Examples from everyday life work because their familiarity to the audience will mean they form rich mental representations for the presenter to build on.

Recently a web-design company was putting together a presentation to give to a potential customer. One of the points they wished to make was that the standard of their work was very high due to the combination of artistic and technical talent that their designers possessed.

They did, of course, appreciate the need for citing examples, and applied the 'spectacular/familiar' guideline. So, from the spectacular point of view, they chose two of their highest profile clients – one a large bank, and the other an Irish folk singer. These may or may not have been the very best websites they had done, but they were certainly engaging examples for the audience. Applying the familiar guideline, when they were later discussing their technical services, they focused on those most accessible to the audience (e-mail, web, online sales) and steered clear of some of the more obscure features they had implemented. The aim was to use familiar examples that would most likely resonate with the needs of the audience.

The 'nine o'clock news' principle – This principle is quite straightforward. As mentioned earlier in the 'To try' in Chapter 7, if you watch the television news with the sound turned down, you will realise that a great many of the images used are not required at all. Most of the images aren't actually doing any direct work in the communication process, but they are still present. The same approach can be applied to the use of examples: if you *can* use an example then you *should* use an example. Always try to show the abstract concept you are talking about and the simplest way to do this is with a generous scattering of examples. These will illustrate your concepts in the same way that the pictures illustrate a news story. Even if the example you have for a particular point is neither very spectacular nor very familiar, any example is better than none at all.

***The Antiques Road Show* principle** – There is a television programme that has been running on the BBC for many years called *The Antiques Road Show*. It has always occupied the same slot on early Sunday evening and the format has not changed in that time. For those who haven't seen it, it is a show where members of the public bring in their antiques to be viewed by a panel of experts. The show goes around the country to a different location each week and people from that region queue up to show the experts their treasures, the most remarkable of which are featured on the programme. What is interesting, though, is the final detail in all of these reviews, the detail everyone has been waiting for: What is it worth?

Value is a kind of bottom line, a standard on which all items can be compared. Of course, for the owner, the charm and personal history of the piece will usually overshadow the price-tag, but it does act as a datum. In the same way, when you are using examples in a presentation, you should try to ground them. Make them as tangible as possible. Giving the cost is only one way of doing this. Let's say you are demonstrating a new model of mobile phone; on top of telling the audience about the new features and advanced technology, you must give them the facts that will make the example real, such as cost, size, weight, when it will be available, where you get it, and so on.

In the case of the Tacoma Narrows Bridge example cited earlier, it would be important to tell the audience where the bridge was (Washington state Olympic Peninsula, USA) when it was built (July 1940), when it collapsed (November 1940), how much it cost ($6 million), and even such details as how many more cars used the bridge than predicted due to the novelty of its wobble (three times) and what the bridge was nicknamed as a result ('Galloping Gertie'). Like a good story, a good example benefits from the sharp definition brought about by details.

Standard weights and measures of the mind: Picture the following scene. You are on holidays in Stockholm, Sweden. You go into a café and order a coffee. You stay for ten minutes, enjoying the ambience and sipping your drink. You then wish to leave so you call the waiter over and ask him, with the aid of some confusing gestures, how much you owe. He tells you in English that it costs 28 Swedish Crowns. You fumble for the right notes and coins, add a tip and give the waiter the money. As you walk out into the street, you return the rest of your money to your pocket. You work out, some ten or twenty seconds later, that twenty eight Swedish Crowns is about €3, and that this is actually quite expensive for a cup of coffee, now that you come to think of it.

We have all experienced this, if not with money then with centimetres and inches, miles and kilometres, pounds and kilograms. We all have our own basic units for measuring the world around us, very like the basic-level associations in the chapter on analogies (naming apples apples, and bananas bananas). And these can be much more complex than weights and measures. Technicians and engineers will often view the same system in very different terms; the technicians from a practical viewpoint, the engineers from the theoretical. In the same way, an audience will have certain direct mental associations and if you can express your examples in those terms, then they will be much easier to mentally integrate. In other words, you must do the currency conversion for them.

Obviously, you cannot know what way each and every audience member will want to digest their facts and figures, but you can at least try to meet them halfway. A good example of this process at work can be seen in any popular science television programme, particularly those on the Discovery Channel. Here the target audience is the general public, so measurements need to be expressed in forms generally meaningful to them. This can be done by making measurements comparative rather than absolute. So, out go the SI units of measurement (metres, kilograms, seconds) and in comes a totally new set of standards. The standard unit of weight or length is the Jumbo Jet. The standard unit of area is the football pitch. The standard unit of volume, and sometimes length, is the double-decker bus, and the standard unit of electrical current is the current necessary to power a light bulb/house/city.

Figure 15.3. Comparative quantities can mean more than absolute ones. The area of a football pitch or the length of a Jumbo Jet will be quantities that most people are familiar with. It is important to match the terms of reference to your audience.

This process, although sometimes bordering on the absurd (e.g. 'enough cable to circle the earth 300 times') is very clever. Absolute numbers often require further calculation to give them a context. But you can do this calculation for the audience. For example, you might say that you have made €755,000 profit in the first quarter of the year, to which your audience might be thinking: 'So what?' But by also mentioning that this is an increase of 20% on the same quarter last year, and exceeds the plan for the year by 10%, and that you are the only company in this sector to have improved profits in this time, then you will bring the raw figure to life. The audience now knows how to interpret this number so that it has real meaning.

A final point about examples is that they tend to be very memorable. When a few working engineers were asked to explain in simplest terms what the Coriolis force was to engineering students, the responses were short and varied. Nine of the 11 responses were incorrect, some wildly so, but the really interesting thing was the plethora of examples that appeared in the responses, citing rotation of the earth, turbo-machinery, spinning tops, magnetic fields, flow-meters, eddy currents, roller-coasters,

To try:

Examples should easily come to mind for a topic in which you are the expert. However these will more than likely be 'local' examples from the immediate domain of the presentation. If you were describing the new computer system, you might refer to the old system, or you might mention tasks that people would typically carry out on the new system in their day-to-day jobs. Sometimes a 'remote' example, from a domain far removed from the one in which you are presenting, can be very engaging too. So, for example, you might be talking about the same computer system and you might describe how it is also used in a particular supermarket chain to control stock levels.

List all of the key points in the presentation. For each, think up one local example and one remote example. You may not use all of these, but you will certainly use some of them.

Key points:

Examples make abstract ideas real. You should use tangible examples whenever you can.

The best examples to use are the very spectacular, or the very familiar.

Relate examples in terms most accessible to the particular audience.

gyroscopes, turntables, a man running, transformers, baths, weather systems, the polar magnetic field, plug-holes, gravity and Coke.

It seems that even though most people had forgotten exactly what the Coriolis force was – or more likely had not understood it in the first place – they still remembered the related examples, even at times a specific drawing or story from a lecture. Examples are a powerful aid to memory. They are a great way of dredging up the content of a presentation: if you remember the example, you can then piece the concept back together. In this way, an example acts like a mental hook, holding up some part of the theory in a way that is memorable.

16. DEMONSTRATIONS

Easily the most underrated and under-utilised of all of the communication tools is the demonstration. The stock-in-trade of conjuring acts, science classes and cookery programmes, the humble demonstration has found little outlet in the rarefied world of the business presentation. In some cases, this is down to a lack of imagination on the part of the presenter. In others, it seems that presenters don't want to get their hands dirty (metaphorically or physically) and want to keep things polished (often a euphemism for 'dull') at all times. In both cases, a really powerful communication tool is being ignored.

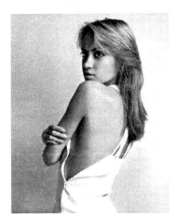

Figure 16.1. You wouldn't buy clothes without trying them on, or a car without test driving it. A demonstration gives the audience a chance to consider your ideas in more detail and on more levels, in effect to try them on. This provides a much richer communication than just words alone.

The main reason why a demonstration works is that it is more engaging than a description or a picture of the same thing. It is in front of you in three dimensions. The presenter might show the device actually working, or might pass it around the audience during the presentation or leave for people to come up and examine at the end. The people in the audience might even get to use it. The fact that it impinges on your memory in more ways than, say, a picture, means that your brain will form a richer mental representation of the event and it will be more memorable as a result. Psychologists refer to this as *elaborative encoding*. It is like the difference between seeing a television programme about New York and actually visiting the place yourself.

In the same way as with examples, demonstrations make abstract ideas real. But there is another important advantage in using demonstrations that most people overlook. This was brought home by an engrossing presentation on the science of rowing. The presenter was a cox for a rowing team and just before she was due to start, the door of the room was thrown open and in came two burly rowers carrying a fairly bulky rowing machine.

One of her assistants sat into the rowing machine and started to row, stopping at various points in the stroke on the instruction of the presenter. She used this working model to discuss concepts of energy, friction and drag, efficiency, force and even team management and communication. There were no slides, no 3-D images or fancy graphics, no bullet points. To produce all of the necessary visual aids would have taken considerable time and effort, a lot more than it took this group to take the rowing machine out of the gym, throw it into the boot of a car and drive it across to where the presentation was being made. And what's more, this 3-D working model was far more engaging than any number of images on a screen. Demonstrations can often considerably reduce your workload.

But she went further. When she was describing the movement of the oars in the water, she extended her arms out on either side of her body and was able to demonstrate all of the main issues: the angular pitch of the paddles, the sweep of the stroke, the lift and drop of the oars into the water. This, as demonstrations go, is as cheap and cheerful as it gets, and yet it was effective.

In regard to visual aids, you must start by asking the question, 'What do I want to achieve at this point?' This too will guide you as to whether a demonstration would best suit your needs and which one to use. Presenters can become so obsessed with the slide-show that they often don't think of doing this, but you should use demonstrations whenever you can.

Literal and representational demonstrations – This is, in some ways, the equivalent to the difference between 'local' and 'remote' examples. A 'literal' demonstration is one where you show what you are talking about: the new model of a product, a broken specimen from a lab test, a computer program.

A 'representational' demonstration, on the other hand, is one where you demonstrate a principle or concept. This takes a bit more imagination. In one presentation, a deck of cards was used to demonstrate principles of probability and statistics. In another, the presenter got the whole room of a few hundred people to split into small groups and answer questions in order to demonstrate certain principles of group dynamics and communication. In another – a necessarily smaller group this time – a matchbox with panels cut out of the sides was used to demonstrate certain principles of structural rigidity.

Presenters are often reluctant to use demonstrations because they can seem a bit rough and messy. You should never adopt this attitude. If you go to the trouble of putting together an interesting demonstration, the audience will usually be fascinated. Always remember: listening is hard work and a creative demonstration can excite great curiosity. It is also likely to be one of the things that the audience remembers.

Stage management – The biggest fault, and it occurs almost always to a greater or lesser extent, is the 'under-demonstration' of demonstrations. People tend not to be deliberate enough and slow enough when they are showing things to the audience. Quite often, presenters hold up items casually as they continue to talk, and the featured demonstration has all the importance of a set of car keys or a fountain pen that the presenter just happens to have in his or her hand. All the time that this is going on, the audience are trying to fix on the object in the way a baby would follow a rattle. They will eventually become frustrated and give up.

Figure 16.2. When showing something, do so very clearly and very slowly. The audience will be seeing this for the first time and will need longer than you imagine to visually examine what you are showing them. Most presenters 'under-demonstrate'.

To try:

Many people worry about demonstrations going wrong. Don't let this put you off. Work out a back-up plan for each one in case things get stuck. The last thing you want to do is draw attention to a demonstration going wrong, but if you have something to move on to, the audience will hardly notice the problem. Just go to your next slide, example, question, story, and get on with it.

Demonstrations can be in view for as little as one or two seconds. This is not nearly enough. You should follow the example of the air stewardess putting on a life jacket before take-off or the magician ostentatiously showing that there is nothing in his hand. Show it for what seems to you an uncomfortably long time, and make the effort to hold it up for everyone in the audience to see. They will be seeing this item for the first time and you need to give them a good few seconds to visually explore it. For many presenters, a gaping pause in a presentation is an unnerving thing. You should, however, not be afraid to do this. Watch the audience when they are watching the demonstration. If most of them are still looking at the object, then they are not yet ready for you to continue. Only when they start to look back at you is it reasonable to continue.

Another important consideration is how you let the audience explore the item for themselves. When showing a visual aid, you can display it when the audience is ready to see it, and you can then remove it when you are finished. But how do you do the same with a demonstration that you wish to pass around? There is no easy answer to this, especially with a larger group. Make a common-sense judgment. You may show the item and then tell the audience that they can look at it after the presentation. Or you may decide to take a break at this point while an item is being passed around. You could take questions at the same time. Whatever you do, don't be afraid to take full control of the situation.

Figure 16.3. There will be a 'what happens next' interest associated with even the simplest demonstrations that will nearly always grab the attention of your audience.

16. Demonstrations

One presenter tackled the problem of using a practical demonstration with a big audience in a very inventive way. He was giving a thermodynamics lecture to a class of about 250 students in a large lecture theatre. He wished to demonstrate the concept of latent heat of evaporation and was using a kettle, a thermometer and a stopwatch to do so. Obviously out of such a large group, only a handful would be able to see what was going on. So he connected a video camera to his laptop by means of a special cable and projected the image on to the overhead screen. Now everyone in the lecture theatre could follow what was going on.

You may be thinking that watching a kettle boil does not make for an event worthy of all of this effort. However, the lecturer had asked the students to write down answers to a few questions in advance. So as the experiment progressed, they were primed to what was going on and interested in the outcome. There is a kind of theatre associated with even a simple demonstration like this. It is a live event, and there is always that uncertainty about what will happen. Even the act of taking something out of a box or lifting it up from under the desk arouses some curiosity in an audience.

Virtual demonstrations – Sometimes it is not possible to bring a demonstration into a presentation, even with the kind of video link-up described above. The next best thing is a *virtual demonstration.* This might be a video clip or a computer-generated animation. This also acts as a change of pace and direction in the presentation, which freshens things up. There are many video clips now available through the internet.

The lesson in all of this is to think beyond the 2-D world of the overhead projector. It is worth reflecting that a presentation affords you an opportunity to demonstrate things firsthand that other communication media don't allow.

Key points:

Demonstrations are more immediate and more effective than visual aids, and usually demand only a fraction of the preparation time.

Presenters usually 'under-demonstrate'. Take plenty of time to let everyone in the audience see what you are showing them.

Think of ways to use representational as well as literal demonstrations.

17. STORIES

It has been established that, through your experience of conversation, you already possess the skills you need to make an engrossing presentation. This point is never more true than in the case of stories. In fact, stories are such an innate part of everyday communication that people often overlook this powerful tool and fail to bring it into their presentations.

Figure 17.1. Stories are the primary way that human beings order, remember and communicate their experiences. From a young age stories hold a magical spell on us, and will capture the attention of your audience, as well as lodging in their memories.

A few years ago a BBC documentary looked at the scientific reasons for the sinking of the Kursk submarine in August 2000. After a mysterious explosion, this vessel sank to the bottom of the Barents Sea on the northern coast of Russia. At the time, it was thought that there were survivors trapped in the hull and there ensued a frantic international effort to get them out. Nine days later, the submarine was finally opened but it was completely flooded and none of the 118 crew were found alive. To this day, the exact cause of the sinking is unknown. The programme explored the most likely reasons for this and used interesting tools to communicate these ideas.

Many examples, analogies, demonstrations and stories were featured, but stories were by far the most heavily used. This is usually the case in television. Although ostensibly a science programme, stories engage human interest and, in a medium that is striving to keep the attention of the general viewer, the story angle will always take centre stage. So there were accounts of 'Lieutenant Dimitri' penning a tragic farewell note to his fiancée, 'Olga', as the submarine was sinking. There was the story of the captain walking up the bridge of the vessel and carrying out various activities on the morning of the disaster. There was also an account of faults incurred by British submarines in the 1950s, and how this could possibly form a connection to the modern disaster. There were, in all, 20 stories during the 45-minute programme.

Later that month 63 presentations took place as part of students' final-year projects. The contrast with the BBC documentary couldn't have been more stark. There were only seven anecdotes in all of the student presentations, even counting those as short as 10 or 20 seconds long, along the lines of: 'I rang the supplier about getting more of the titanium alloy but he said it was out of stock for the next six weeks, so he suggested we use a nickel alloy…'; anything at all that told of an event and referred to real people. Amazingly, only seven stories in total were used in all the student presentations.

You may say this is an unreasonable comparison. Television is there to entertain and presentations are there to inform. This is true, but the powerful story tool shouldn't just be discarded altogether. Pay attention on your next coffee or lunch break with work colleagues, and you should observe that the conversation is one long exchange of stories:

> *Story 1* – *'Did you see they're shutting down their operation in the west?'*

> *Story 2* – *'That's interesting, I was talking to a guy who used to work there and he told me that…'*

> *Story 3* – *'Yes, it'll be a bit more difficult for us now. I remember before when…'*

> *Story 4* – *'What we could do is… John was telling me about…'*

Stories are the way we package experiences. To form a story we pluck a few events out of a constant stream of experiences and perceptions and package them into a coherent structure. And the amazing thing is that we do this effortlessly. It is a standard human template and as such it is easy for the listener to understand and remember.

Say a friend returns from a holiday in America. He has been away for two weeks. If you ask him how it went, he is unlikely to say, 'Well I took off on the third of May. The weather was clement and I was in a relaxed frame of mind. I had a drink. Then I had some dinner. Then I watched a film…' This would be fairly boring. It is more likely that his reply will be along the lines of, 'Oh you would have loved it, we went to this baseball game…' if you were interested in sport. Out of all his experiences and perceptions over the period of the holiday, he would extract enough details to construct just the stories that are relevant to you.

The boundaries of a story can be rearranged to suit a different task or audience. We can look at a set of incidents and see that, organised in a certain way, they form an interesting pattern that is worth remembering. So why had the students been so reluctant to use stories? Well, one reason might be that younger people aren't quite as adept at telling stories as older people. It is one of those communication skills that we go on developing throughout our lives. Children, even young teenagers, can be positively awful at telling stories. However, these students were all in their early twenties and many of them seemed well able to communicate confidently and clearly. And even professional engineers, some with many years of experience, are quite often loathe to include stories in their presentations. There seems to be something else fundamental that discourages presenters from telling stories – maybe it is a feeling that the personal has no part in a technical presentation.

This attitude is very foolish. All work is carried out by people, for people. The central point of the kind of story you might use in a presentation is not an emotional or spiritual truism, as it might be in the stories of literature or cinema. These are stories relating the experiences of an expert, who has worked in a particular area, and as such are invaluable to the audience. They are packages of experience in the form: 'I remember one time…'; 'We experienced this before…'; 'I'll never forget that episode…'

Stories and Eyewitness Testimony

One interesting piece of 'evidence' that shows the powerful packaging effect of a story comes from a set of studies carried out by Elizabeth Loftus, a renowned researcher in the field of memory, on what affects the memories of witnesses in court. She posed the question, 'How much weight does the jury place on the testimony of eyewitnesses?' The result of these experiments throws up an interesting insight into how memorable stories are.

A mock-trial experiment was carried out in which people were asked to play the roles of jurors, listen to testimony and reach a verdict. The mock jurors were given a description of a grocery store robbery in which the owner and his granddaughter were killed. They received a summary of the evidence and arguments presented at the defendant's trial and then each juror was asked to arrive at a verdict of guilty or not guilty. The mock jurors were split into three groups (unknown to themselves). The trial information that each of the three groups received was identical except for one key detail:

- The first group was told that there were no eyewitnesses to the crime.
- The second group was told that a store clerk had testified that he had seen the defendant shoot the two victims, although the defence attorney had, of course, disputed this.
- The third group had also heard the claims of the store clerk witness but the defence attorney had discredited him by showing that the clerk had not been wearing his glasses on the day of the robbery and that his eyesight was too poor to allow him to see the face of the robber from where he stood.

The jurors were then asked to give their verdicts on the guilt of the defendant. The differences between the verdicts given by the three groups are revealing. In the first group, where there had been no eyewitnesses, 18% of the jurors thought that the defendant was guilty. In the second group, with the addition of a single witness, the conviction rate rose to 72%. Interestingly, in the third group, for whom the eyewitness had been substantially impeached, 68% of the jurors still voted to convict.

It would seem that eyewitness testimony carries considerable weight. This idea is reinforced by a further experiment, which compared the strength of eyewitness testimony with other forms of evidence. In this case, the defendant passed a forged cheque in order to purchase a television set. Four groups of mock jurors were given the same account of the trial except in regard to one key piece of testimony. One group was given an eyewitness account, a second group saw a handwriting analysis that linked the accused to the crime, the third was presented with a fingerprint match and the final group was presented with a positive polygraph lie detector test. The group of jurors who received the eyewitness account had the highest rate of convictions (78%), compared with all other pieces of testimony: fingerprint (70%), polygraph (53%), and handwriting (34%).

How does this relate to the use of stories in presentations? Stories are a powerful communication tool because they are engaging, coherent and memorable. When a witness to a crime stands up in court to tell his story, he presents a smooth, unified account, which can be easily stored in the memories of the jurors. On the other hand, evidence that is presented in pieces, from different sources and at different times, must be reconstructed by the jurors, which requires far more cognitive effort.

Figure 17.2. One of the reasons that eyewitness testimony is so persuasive is that the witness presents their evidence as a single coherent account (a story) rather than a set of propositions and facts scattered throughout the trial.

This should be remembered when presenting. You should never just present a litany of facts and figures and expect your audience to piece these together in the desired way. Instead, you should present as if you are telling a story. Be the eyewitness for your own material, personalising your account, building up a logical narrative and reaching a sensible conclusion. For your audience, this will be more interesting, easier to follow and, above all, more memorable.

Indeed, the eyewitness effect is used in the news all the time. During a recent spell of particularly heavy rain, one district in Dublin city had been badly flooded. This story was newsworthy because so much rain had fallen on such a large area and affected so many people. However, the focus on the news that day wasn't on these broad statistics, but rather on the individual cases that brought these statistics to life. There was a woman whose kitchen was under three feet of water, a shop-owner whose entire stock had been ruined, a pensioner who had to be rescued from her house and the eyewitness account of a fireman who had never seen anything like it before.

These items are not in themselves newsworthy. If you flood your kitchen tomorrow, don't expect CNN to cover the event, however distressing it is for you. The stories are newsworthy only because they are symptomatic of a larger and more remarkable problem. However, the individual stories are used to provide coherent accounts that put the larger problem into perspective. The listeners can understand what two inches of rain in eight hours really means when related in this way. Stories allow us to make direct comparisons with our own experiences. In this regard, they are like analogies, and are therefore very compelling and useful.

The overall lesson regarding stories should be clear by now. They work in two ways. Firstly, they are a natural memory package and so are likely to stay in the memory of the audience. Secondly, they capture the audience's attention; simply put, everyone loves a good story. You should not be afraid to share your experiences with your audience, in the same way that you would if you were in conversation with them as individuals. This may seem like a bit of an indulgence at first, but it is too useful a communication tool to ignore.

It is worth echoing this with the words of one of the most famous presentation skills coaches of all time: Dale Carnegie. Carnegie first published his ideas on how to present in 1920 and this work (now under the title *The Quick and Easy Way to Effective Speaking*) has been selling ever since. He said of his most famous work, *How to Win Friends and Influence People*, 'The rules from *How to Win Friends and Influence People* can be listed on one-and-a-half pages. The other 230 pages are filled with stories and illustrations to point up how others have used these rules with wholesome effect.'

You will have noticed that there is no set of guidelines in this section on how to best use stories for communication, as was done with the other three tools. This is because storytelling is such an innate ability that it is very hard to analyse the craft objectively. Of the four

To try:

When you become more comfortable as a speaker, you can try the following to demonstrate the power of stories. Very deliberately begin a story in your talk and watch the reaction of the group. You will find that even those who have been scribbling or attending to something else will look up to hear the story. You will notice that the whole atmosphere in the room changes. Everyone will be wondering the same thing: 'What happened?'

A further twist to this exercise is to leave out some final detail. For example, you may be talking about a mistake some employee made that led to a big loss for his company. You might logically conclude things should be carried out in a certain way to avoid such problems. However, you might also deliberately decline to say what became of the luckless employee. If you then pause at the end of the story, or even ask if there are any questions, it's highly likely someone in the audience will ask you to clarify this.

tools looked at, stories have been by far the hardest to research. It is next to impossible to tell someone how best to construct a story, despite – and probably because of – the fact that you have been doing this every conscious moment of your life, even when you are not speaking. We construct stories to make sense of our experiences, and we tell stories to pass this sense on to others. With something that is so much a part of how we think and communicate, why on earth would you not use stories in your presentations?

PART FIVE: BRINGING IT ALL TOGETHER

This last part examines how to put all of the things covered in this book into practice. These are things you do before and after the presentation to get the most out of what you have prepared. There is also a chapter (20) looking at some specialised presentation tasks that many people are faced with at one time or another.

18. PLANNING THE OVERALL PROCESS

This check-list will help you to answer all of the key questions before you start. If you follow this planning process, it should ensure a clean line of logic through your presentation.

Title –

Time –

Target audience –

Aim – What are you trying to achieve with the presentation? You must ask the question: What do you want your audience to do as a result of the talk?

Approach – The aim spells out what you are going to do for your audience in the presentation; the approach describes how you are going to achieve this. It is essentially a tactical plan that states, in a few sentences, the logical route through your presentation to achieve this goal.

Script – This is a plan for your presentation. In other words, when you decide what approach you are going to take, you are then in a position to draw up a step-by-step plan of each item that will be in the talk. Don't forget to include an effective introduction and a memorable conclusion.

Slide sentences – For every visual aid that you use, you should be able to write a single sentence that describes what function the slide is carrying out.

Tools – Try to use as many communication tools as possible. Analogies, examples, stories and demonstrations are excellent ways of packaging information so that it is digestible and memorable for the audience. Try to be imaginative in how you explain concepts. For each item in your talk, ask yourself the question, 'Is there another way that I could explain this?'

Check the Venue

This should be obvious, but in practice, it doesn't seem to be. People arrive just before they are due to speak with CDs that won't read, or memory sticks that won't install, and then look at the host accusingly. To walk to the front of a room with an intention to just plug in and get going is crazy. People worry themselves into a terrible state over having to make a presentation, sometimes for many weeks prior to the actual event, and then risk ruining the talk for want of a few minute's preparation.

When things go wrong, there is only one person who looks foolish and that is you. It may not be your fault, but it is definitely your problem. All excuses are null and void.

You should arrive in plenty of time and check everything that you need to. Do so the day before if you can. You will sleep better on the eve of a presentation if you have been in the venue and seen it for yourself. If this is not possible, and you are unsure of something, then ring the organisers and ask them about it. You have to be a bit like a demanding celebrity when it comes to these things. It's your show, and only you will suffer if things go wrong.

You might be reading this and thinking that it all makes perfect sense, but in practice, it is not always possible to check things in advance, or to arrive early to the venue. Also, you may be following immediately after another presenter, with very little time for the changeover. However, there are always ways around this. You can ring the organisers in advance, and eliminate many possible pitfalls before you travel. Presenters usually feel passive in the whole process, that they can only turn up and do their best, and if there are things out of their control, then there's little that can be done. This is not the case. Most organisers will welcome your queries in advance of the presentation as it will help ensure the smooth running of the event they are staging.

Something else that may not be possible, but which will greatly help, is to meet the people who will be in the audience beforehand. This will reduce the fear factor considerably and it will probably make the audience more responsive as they will have had a chance to see that you are human too. Even if you can't meet them face to face, you may be able to correspond with them in advance of the talk. This not only breaks the ice, but it allows you to find out a bit more about your audience, which will help you to better tailor the material to their needs.

Get Feedback

If you give someone a document and ask them to review it for you, they will hand it back covered in red marks and scribbles and you will thank them for their input. If, however, you walk up to someone after you have given a presentation and ask them what they thought of it, they'll probably turn white as a sheet and mumble all sorts of awkward encouragements, especially if it wasn't very good. And, on the off-chance that they are honest, you will probably resent the criticism.

We are not used to criticising presentations. The whole business is taken very personally and as such it is hard to get any decent feedback at all. You can be clever about this. You might ask someone what messages they took away from the talk and compare them to your aims. You might say to them, 'I got a bit rushed towards the end and I don't remember what I was doing. I was probably a bit unclear at that point. Did you notice?' By criticising yourself in this way, you will disarm any criticism that they wish to make and you might get a useful insight, for example, 'No, it was pretty clear really. The only thing I noticed is that you said "basically" quite a few times.'

There are lots of cunning ways to invite honest feedback. You can also give out a questionnaire at the end, although often you won't have the time to do this. Be careful, however, as there are many people with a poor understanding of the process who will gladly offer you advice.

Practise

You have to give presentations in order to become a polished presenter. Seek opportunities to present and to put the various lessons in this book into practice. The main thing practise will do is to accustom you to the feeling of being in front of an audience. With each presentation the strangeness will subside and you will be able to devote more of your attention to the task in hand. Many people who have speak at a wedding are thrown by the sound of their own voice over the microphone and the ripples of laughter in the audience. Wedding crowds are extremely generous with their laughter, but it can still be unnerving when they laugh loud and long at things the speaker didn't intend to be funny, and not at all at the things they did.

With practise, however, you know how to make the necessary adjustments. Stan Laurel said that he would have re-edited all of the Laurel and Hardy films for television because the original cuts had pauses to match the long communal laughter of the cinema, but this meant that the films were improperly paced for television. In a presentation, you can re-edit on the spot, but only if you are practised enough to observe a situation and know how to adjust accordingly.

Key point:

Very thorough planning and preparation are vital in ensuring the successful delivery of a presentation.

19. DEALING WITH QUESTIONS

Questions are the only thing you cannot script in advance, and for this reason are often greatly feared by presenters. However, they are usually the most stimulating part of the event, and as such, should be welcomed and prepared for. The following are the most important things to keep in mind.

Figure 19.1. The question-and-answer session after the presentation, although feared by many presenters, is often the most effective and engaging part.

Be nice – However edgy you may feel, be nice to the questioner. Remember that they are speaking in front of the group as well, and will possibly be more nervous than you are. Don't be short or smart in any way, even if you suspect the questioner is trying to catch you out. If you come down hard on one member of the audience, the whole audience will feel slighted.

The question-and-answer session at the end of a presentation is often the best part of the overall communication. It allows a dialogue between the expert and interested attendees. Also, if you go to the trouble of preparing and delivering a long presentation and no one asks a single question when you finish, you will probably be far more deflated than relieved.

Prepare for questions – You would not go into a job interview without rehearsing answers to probable questions, and you should do the same for a presentation. If you get someone to assist you it will really help.

Don't interrupt – Some presenters jump in with an answer as soon as they get a whiff of something they can talk about. Be it due to nerves or enthusiasm, it is massively annoying and disrespectful, and you will probably not satisfy the need that provoked the question. The brave questioner will force you to try again; the shy one will resign unfulfilled. Listen patiently and respectfully to the question – the whole question.

Repeat the question – The reason for doing this is twofold. Firstly, it is likely – in all but the cosiest venues – that some of the audience won't have heard the question properly. Secondly, it enables you to clarify what the question is. Some presenters overdo this. It sounds very obsequious to always begin your answers with, 'Thank you for your excellent question. The lady in the front row has just inquired if…' and so forth, so use your common sense. If the room is small enough, just answer the question.

Take questions throughout – Some people like to keep in control until the end, then take questions. They worry that if they allow questions during the talk, they could go way over time. However, it is a good idea, in a longer presentation, to factor in some time for questions as you go along. When the audience are asking questions, they are involved, and the whole event doesn't weigh so heavy. If things get out of hand, you can always politely suggest that you should press on and take up the discussion at the end.

In a long presentation, you might even take a break in the middle and ask for questions. This acts as a nice change of pace and freshens things up. Also, if you go looking for questions at the end, everyone might be ready to leave and they will not be well disposed to ask anything at that stage. Be very careful of this. Even people who do wish to ask a question may let it pass if they see half of their colleagues putting on their jackets and making for the door.

Don't answer if you don't know – You have thought about your audience, decided what you can do for them, spelt this out in the introduction, delivered your well-prepared material clearly and finished with a useful conclusion in the allotted time. Then someone asks you a question, not aligned to this task, and you find you cannot answer it. What do you do? You simply say, 'I don't know.'

If someone went into a shoe shop and asked for aspirin, the shopkeeper would tell him that he couldn't be of assistance. The same is true in a presentation. Don't try to bluff. You are there to do a job, not to know everything there is to know about a subject. If someone asks you about something specific to your talk, for example about the source of data for a particular graph, and you don't know the answer, then you are at fault. But you are not duty-bound to be a fountain of knowledge on every related topic.

If possible, you may volunteer to look into it and get back to the questioner. One excellent example of this was demonstrated by a keynote speaker at a conference, when he was asked a question for which he did not have an answer and which probably wasn't relevant to the needs of most of the audience. His response was, 'I don't have an answer to that right now, but there's a colleague of mine who probably does. If you can write the question on the back of a business card and give it to me after the presentation, I'll look into it when I'm back in the office next week and e-mail an answer to you.' This handled the situation perfectly: he dealt with the questioner's need, prevented the situation from upsetting his progress unnecessarily, and was polite and urbane while doing so.

Talk to the whole audience – If you decide the question is worth answering, then it is worth answering for everyone and you should look at everyone when doing so. Crucially, as you reach the end of your response, look back in the direction of the questioner and, if you wish, ask them if this answers their question.

Don't over-answer – This is usually done by the same type of person who interrupts the questioner. It is extremely annoying. A presenter will start to speak, and then their enthusiasm will carry them on to related points, and the answer will run on and on. If you do this two or three times, the audience will button up very quickly and that will end the question-and-answer session.

Don't under-answer – This is a bit more rare but it can happen, particularly with very knowledgeable, technical presenters. Technical people, particularly those from a mathematical or scientific background, can quite often see the world in black-and-white terms. When asked a question, they will usually issue as concise an answer as they can. However, at the heart of every question is a need. Often, the question and the need will be identical ('Where do I catch the number 42 bus?'), but this is not always the case. An example of this occurred when the sales manager of a company was asking a senior engineer some questions after the engineer had made a presentation. The sales manager was confused and unhappy about something but he didn't have the expertise, background knowledge, or vocabulary to express this concern. The engineer answered the questions that were put to him as concisely as he could, but he failed to probe the real need that was driving those questions. It is a bit like when someone asks, 'Is anyone going to eat that slice of cake?' when what they really want to ask is, 'Can I have it?'

Don't be afraid to spend time clarifying the question (or, more to the point, the need behind the question) as it can save a lot of bother in the long run. It also shows that you are interested and concerned.

Persistently hostile questioners – If you find that you cannot politely postpone a question, then you are likely under attack from someone with a truly hostile agenda. People ask me about this scenario all the time, even though it happens only very rarely. However, in the event that it does happen, the way to deal with this is first to be patient and stay friendly. Always be nice, or as nice as you can be. Second, try to postpone the question. Tell the person that you would be glad to discuss it with him afterwards, but that you don't really have time to go into it now. If it is a tricky question then it will probably be off the beaten track of the presentation and this will sound totally reasonable.

If he is really intent on shooting you down, however, he will persist. The third step to take is to try to turn the question back on him. Say something like: 'I'm not sure what you want me to say. Maybe you could explain what's confusing you and why you're dissatisfied with my response and then I might be able to help you.' This is really inviting him out into the open. He is trying to make you look like a fool, for whatever reason, and the way he is doing this is by asking you a question that he knows you can't answer. He is effectively forcing you to dig your own grave. But if you turn it back on him, he has to either admit that he is being vindictive or back down. You may even decide to be more direct: 'Why are you asking me this?'

If all of this fails, you can resort to the fourth and final step: demand that he keeps quiet and lets you continue. This kind of hard-handed tactic will normally alienate your audience, but the crucial point here is that the questioner will have had to go so far to reach this point that the audience will probably have disowned him and will now be glad to see him put in his place. Remember, the audience is there to get something useful from you, the expert, and if one loose cannon is pursuing his own agenda, then he is wasting their time.

It should be stressed again that, although this is many presenters' nightmare scenario, it really is very rare. Presentations are like conversations – they are constructive and collaborative, with the presenter and the audience working together to build meaning. It is in their interests for you to be clear and useful. The audience are rooting for you, and will delight in your success.

Let someone else answer – Don't be afraid to bring the audience in. If someone were to ask, 'What is the most common mistake people make when presenting?', a good response would be, 'Well, what do you think?' It is quite likely that a question of this form is asked because the questioner has thought about the issue himself. By bouncing the question back, you are showing respect for the audience as well as getting them involved, which is always a good thing. And when the questioner has offered his or her opinion, you can follow this with something like, 'Well, I do have an answer to this question based on my own experiences but before I share it with you, does anyone else have a strong view on this?'

In a similar vein, you should not be slow to pass the question over to someone else, 'John, you've done a lot of work in this area. How would you respond.' You have to be careful not to put people on the spot, but to be called on in this way is flattering and rarely offends.

20. SPECIAL CASES

There are different types of presentation. Many books list these (technical conference, after-dinner speech, public meeting) and give guidelines for each one, but the same basic principles apply to each, and are addressed as such in this book. However, it is worth mentioning three special cases that deviate a little from the basic assumptions. They are academic lectures, conference presentations, and wedding speeches.

Academic Lectures

All of the lessons discussed in regard to presentations can be applied equally well to giving a lecture: eye contact, style, preparation, visual aids, communication tools. The one big difference is the concept of 'expert' and 'interested group'. A lecturer will certainly be an expert, but a class of students do not fall into the category of 'interested group'.

This is not to disparage the youth of today by saying they are lazy and unfocused. Far from it; students are more worldly and competitive today than they have ever been, and generally take their education very seriously. However, they do not come into each lecture with a specific need that they wish to be addressed. Instead, a general body of material is presented to them, lecture after lecture, week after week. The difference between a presentation and a lecture is like the difference between visiting a doctor for ten minutes to find out what is wrong with you, and visiting a doctor over several months to get all the information on all of the things that could possibly go wrong in the future.

In many ways, this mode of education is slightly absurd. You spend several years telling people how to solve problems that they haven't yet encountered. Most students at the outset of their education don't really know exactly what they will do when they go into the workplace. And yet, this is probably the only feasible way to educate and train people for a profession.

The trick in lecturing is to get the audience interested before you start. Think of the process as getting the students to ask the questions before you answer these questions. It's a sort of priming process. To achieve this, students should be active in the lecture, not passive. The idea of a lecturer speaking nonstop for an hour with students taking notes is far too flat and presenter-focused. If the students are this passive, they simply cannot be learning at any kind of high level and it is naïve to think that they will remember everything you say.

You can set students small tasks in lectures in order to have them formulate the question in their heads before you provide a solution. These tasks may be simply questions that you pose at the outset, but if you also allow some time for the students to try to answer these questions for themselves, thereby processing the problem in a more thorough way, this will enhance the exercise. It is important to point out, however, that the questions or tasks that you pose need not be exam questions or formal problems. At the time you are lecturing students, you are really only in a position to explain concepts. To gain a deep understanding of the material, students will have to go away and spend considerable time going through the material themselves. But if you can arm them with an understanding of some of the concepts that underpin this material, they will be better able to tackle the detailed theory when the time comes.

It can also be very stimulating to have interaction in the lecture between the lecturer and the students. This has to be handled carefully, however. Picking out individual students and asking them questions is a little too aggressive and will result in a lot of stony non-responses and fear. And if you simply allow students to volunteer answers, you will probably only get responses from a handful of the more confident people in the class.

One way around this problem is to set short exercises or questions to groups. Get the students to form into small groups in whatever way is convenient from where they are sitting. Then allow them to discuss the problem among themselves and arrive at an agreed response from each group. This works well for several reasons: the weaker students learn from the stronger ones; the stronger students learn by having to articulate and explain their answers to the others; and everyone in the class is contributing answers, but without being put on the spot. All opinions get canvassed. The answers can then form the basis of a discussion, or can be collected by the lecturer and fed back to the students in the next class. This has the added benefit of alerting the lecturer to gaps that occur repeatedly in the students' answers, or of the angles taken in the exercise that the lecturer may not have thought of himself.

Lecturing is difficult because of the fundamental problem of having to get your audience interested and mentally involved. To help you to focus the minds of the class, it is a good idea to set goals at the start of each lecture, and to tell the students what these goals are. It is not good enough to just talk students through notes, or worse, to simply dictate them or display them for the students to write them down. You must ask yourself, 'What can I do in this 40- or 50-minute slot that will best aid the students in the overall learning task outlined in the course syllabus?'

Lecturing is not an easy thing to do well but it is a fascinating, and at times very rewarding, challenge.

Conference Presentations

There is a community of academics across the globe who carry out research and then get together and tell each other what they have done. Simple, right? Yes, but what role does the presentation play in all of this? Surely a detailed technical paper would suffice to tell the world what you have done, and without the considerable bother and expense of taking days away from work and travelling long distances. What can you do in the time you have to present that you couldn't do by any other means? Put another way, what value can you add to the publication of your research by presenting it in this way?

This leads you into a different way of thinking about the exercise. And yet, most presentations are ordered in exactly the same way as the technical paper on which they are based: background, equipment, testing, results, conclusions and future work. Remember the two introductory slides shown in Figure 5.2, which were taken from consecutive conference presentations. You might feel that this generic structure is perfectly logical, but by doing this, you are selecting the structure before you have decided what you wish the presentation to achieve. Instead, examine the aim first.

If your aim is to tell the rest of the community what you have found, the presentation should be ordered in such a way as to bring this message cleanly to the audience. You should start with your conclusions. Tell them what you've found, and then go into the details of how this was achieved, fleshing out the details and explaining the assumptions you made along the way. Don't wait until the end to draw conclusions – just because the conclusions came at the end of your research work, this doesn't mean they have to come at the end of your presentation on it. If the audience don't know at the start where you are going to take them, then how will they know if they should tag along?

Another reason to present is to establish credibility or raise your profile among the academic community. Indeed, this aim might run in parallel with the one above. Again, if you are aware of this aim, it will guide you as to what to include and what to leave out of the talk. Ask precise questions. For instance, what do you wish to publicise about your work and why? Are you putting yourself forward as a potential research partner to those present? Are you looking to recruit? Are you looking for funding? Are you simply looking to make contacts? If so, have you brought additional handout material, business cards and contact details? Have you informed those present how you wish to follow up the presentation?

On this note, another reason to present is simply to provoke discussion. One very powerful aspect of all presentations is the fact that you have the expert there in person and you can interact with this expert. (This is not the case with a technical paper, obviously.) So do you wish this to be the focus of the presentation? If so, have you built in time at the end to take these questions? Have you communicated to the audience, clearly, that their participation is desired? Have you organised a forum for a follow-up discussion at a later stage?

Only with a clear aim are you in a position to structure a conference presentation in a sensible way.

Wedding Speeches

Much has been written and said about wedding speeches, but, true to the logic outlined in this book, the key thing to figure out is what you wish to achieve. For the target audience, what function are you fulfilling?

There are really three:

1. Welcoming people
2. Thanking people
3. Entertaining the crowd

The first function is obvious. You are saying a communal hello and welcome to everyone present. You might also be telling people who's who. This makes sense, as most people will only be acquainted with one side of the family. It is courteous to welcome people in this way, and is a fairly straightforward task.

The second aim is, arguably, a bit dubious. If you wish to thank someone for doing the flowers or making the cake, then it is probably far more sincere to walk up to him, look him in the eye and say 'thank you'. Saying it in front of the assembly is, possibly, a bit ostentatious. However, this is what people have come to expect and so you may just have to play ball. Make a list. This is where guide notes are vital. If you do go down the route of thanking people and you leave someone out, it is embarrassing for both of you.

The last point is the most well-known feature of the speeches and is pretty daunting. In many ways, the crowd expect 10 minutes of stand-up comedy, and people organising weddings can be very inflexible about all of this. They feel they are expected to follow tradition and they do this blindly with the result that ordinary people, many of whom are petrified about speaking in public, have to do so in front of a crowd of possibly hundreds and be entertaining into the bargain. Seen in this way, the whole thing is positively barbaric.

Figure 20.1. Although one of the main (and somewhat daunting) briefs for a speaker at a wedding is to be funny, if you are not used to making presentations, restrict yourself to telling a few personal, tasteful stories. A wedding crowd will laugh at nearly anything.

That said, the tradition will continue. So how should you go about making a wedding speech? The answer should be obvious. It's the communication tool that people have been using for years: stories. Pick two or three stories. If you are the best man, tell a couple of stories about the groom and at least one that involves the bride. Don't worry about being funny – if you have picked out an interesting story then it will be funny by default. A wedding crowd is the easiest audience you will ever speak in front of; they will laugh at absolutely anything.

As to whether you should tell a mortifying story about the groom: you shouldn't. Not only does it mortify the groom, it mortifies the bride even more so, and it's cringingly uncomfortable for both families. You have to ask the question: How much of your target audience are you actually serving by doing this? It is really just the product of an immature best man trying to entertain his friends and little more. It's not saying you shouldn't have a go at the groom, but that doesn't mean you have to disgrace him. Be satirical and irreverent certainly, but not demeaning.

A last point that applies to all speeches, but wedding speeches in particular, is to keep it brief. The greatest failing of the amateur performer is that they go on far too long. Everyone reading this book will have heard of or directly experienced the horror of speeches lasting for literally hours. Again, you have to ask the question: Who does this serve? What part of the target audience profits by all of these speeches? It can be hard to chop material once you have gone to the trouble of writing it, but that's exactly what you must do. So many really brilliant speeches start to eat themselves whole by going on too long. The speaker starts to dissipate his own energy, which is a waste. If you stand up and entertain the crowd for a brief few minutes, say a polite thank you and then sit down; people will think you are a genius, they really will.

FINAL WORD

It has already been said that practise will bring the guidelines in this book to life. It's a process of becoming accustomed to being in the presentation hot-seat and then allowing your natural style into your presentation. When you do this, it is very fulfilling.

If you are really serious about improving your presentation skills, then you should try to be as creative as possible. You have been given the general guidelines for making a presentation, but there are a thousand ways to present anything. Try to get help from other people for brainstorming purposes and be as creative as you can. Also, watch and learn from the example of others, both the good and bad examples.

Finally, you have to take a few risks. The key to really engaging, memorable presentations is to use the communication tools in the last part of the book: analogies, examples, demonstrations and stories. If you use these, and take a small risk or two, audiences will greatly appreciate the effort, and your presentations will be far more interesting and memorable as a result.

READER NOTES

READER NOTES

READER NOTES